GFOA BUDGETING SERIES

Volt

Organization and Design of an Effective Budget Function

R. Gregory Michel

GOVERNMENT FINANCE OFFICERS ASSOCIATION

Copyright 2002 by the Government Finance Officers Association of the
United States and Canada
203 N. LaSalle Street, Suite 2700
Chicago, IL 60601
www.gfoa.org

ISBN no. 0-89125-262-2

Library of Congress control number: 2002107249

Printed in the United States of America.

Contents

Exhibits

Foreword

How to organize the budget function is a topic that is of significant interest to elected officials, public managers, finance officers, and public interest groups. The design of the budget function could very well affect financial outcomes. Despite its importance, there is currently little written on the topic.

This book provides state, provincial, and local governments with a helpful resource for any effort to improve the organization structure and staffing of the budget function. It highlights the advantages and disadvantages of various organizational designs and summarizes the actual structures and responsibilities given to budget offices. As a volume in the GFOA Budgeting Series, the book also provides governments with additional tools and techniques for implementing the recommended practices of the National Advisory Council on State and Local Government (NACSLB).

The GFOA would like to thank the author, R. Gregory Michel, Manager in the GFOA Research and Consulting Center, for writing this publication. We thank the reviewers for their insight and helpful comments: Craig Clifford, Finance Director, City of Scottsdale, Arizona; Eric R. Johnson, Director, Management and Budget Department, Hillsborough County, Florida; and David Y. Miller, Associate Dean and Professor, Graduate School of Public and International Affairs, University of Pittsburgh. Thanks are also due to Rowan Miranda, Director and Nicholas Greifer, Manager, both of the GFOA Research and Consulting

Center, for their many insightful comments. The author wishes to thank Salomon Guajardo, formerly of the GFOA Research and Consulting Center, for the initial idea for the publication and Rebecca Russum for her assistance in publishing this manuscript.

Jeffrey L. Esser
Executive Director
Government Finance Officers Association

CHAPTER 1

Introduction

The design of the budget function is one of the most important organizational issues within state, provincial, and local government. The way the budget function operates has a wide-ranging effect on the budget itself, the budget office, the government as a whole, and even the community. Despite the importance of the organizational design of the budget function, however, there is very little written on the topic.

This book examines key questions pertaining to the responsibilities, design, and staffing of the budget function, including:

- What responsibilities should be given to the budget office?
- Should the budget office be directly under the Chief Financial Officer or the Chief Executive?
- How are budget offices organized internally?
- How can coordination be increased within the budget office? and,
- What skills should a budget analyst have?

As a way of introducing the budgeting function, the following section discusses its multi-faceted nature.

ASPECTS OF THE BUDGETING FUNCTION

The budgeting function in state and local government has many aspects, including: 1) financial, 2) political, 3) planning/analytical, 4) administrative, and 5) communicative. The multifaceted nature of governmental budgeting is widely recognized.[1] According to the National Advisory Council on State and Local Budgeting (NACSLB), "good budgeting is a broadly defined process that has political, managerial, planning, communication, and financial dimensions."[2] The Government Finance Officers Association's (GFOA) Distinguished Budget Presentation Awards Program defines a budget document to be not only a financial plan, but also a policy document, operations guide, and communications device.[3]

Financial Aspect. First and foremost, budgeting is a *financial* activity with the goal of producing a plan for future revenue collection and spending. In fact, the fundamental legal requirement in state and local governmental budgeting is financial, i.e., the budget must be balanced. A typical budget document includes detailed financial information on past and future revenues, expenditures, and fund balance. Through budgeting, revenues and expenditures are estimated; monies are segregated in appropriate funds; and debt service, payroll, and other expenditures are provided for. Financially, the purpose of budgeting is to achieve long-term structural balance between revenues and expenditures.

Political Aspect. Political conflict plays a fundamental role in budgeting because it involves the allocation of scarce resources. Bland and Rubin identify six sources of conflict in the budgeting process (see Exhibit 1-1). One arena of conflict is between department heads, who seek to maximize their department's budget, and the central budget office, which seeks to limit spending in order to balance revenues and expenditures. Related to this conflict is the budget office's need for departmental information in order to cut inefficient or ineffective activities, and departments' need for secrecy in order to prevent cuts in their budget. Another arena of conflict is between the need for accurate revenue estimates and the need of elected officials to maintain a positive financial image. The budget office generally prefers to err on the side of underestimating revenues in order to maintain a balanced budget. An overly conservative estimate, however, could reflect badly on the government's financial condition (and embarrass elected officials). In addition, a smaller "pot" of revenue makes it more difficult for elected officials to satisfy competing interest groups.

The tradeoff between enhancing citizen participation and increasing efficiency through centralization of power and control is another

Exhibit 1-1 ■ Sources of Political Conflict in the Budgeting Process

Conflict	Sides of Conflict	Interests
1. Size of agency budgets	Department heads	Seek to maximize their department's budget.
	Central budget office	Seeks to limit spending in order to balance revenues and expenditures.
2. Departmental information	Department heads	Want to maintain secrecy in order to prevent unnecessary cuts in their budget.
	Central budget office	Want departmental information in order to cut inefficient or ineffective activities.
3. Revenue estimates	Elected officials	Prefer to err on the side of overestimating revenues to give a good impression of the government's future financial condition and make it easier to satisfy competing interest groups.
	Central budget office	Prefers to err on the side of underestimating revenues in order to maintain a balanced budget.
4. Citizen participation versus efficiency	Citizens	Increase democracy through citizen participation.
	Officials	Increase efficiency through centralization of power and control.
5. Special constituencies versus community as a whole	Special constituencies	Policies and services should benefit the specific interests of the constituency.
	Community as a whole	Policies and services should benefit the community as a whole.
6. Direct democracy versus representative democracy	Direct democracy	Decisions should be based on what residents say they want (through hearings, polls, letters, etc.).
	Representative democracy	Decisions should be based on what public officials think that residents really need (based on officials' wisdom and greater access to information).

Source: Based on material that originally appeared in Robert L. Bland and Irene S. Rubin, *Budgeting: A Guide for Local Governments* (Washington, D.C.: International City/County Management Association, 1997), 11-19.

tension in the budget process. Serving the interests of special constituencies versus the interests of the community as a whole represents another area of conflict in the budget process. A sixth source of tension is between what residents say they want (through hearings, polls, letters, etc.), and what public officials think that they really need (based on officials' wisdom and greater access to information). This can be seen as direct democracy (the unmediated preferences of the electorate) versus representative democracy (in which the views of the electorate are transmitted through their elected officials). Politically, the purpose of budgeting is to coordinate and control conflict to the benefit of the entire government.[4]

Planning/Analytical Aspect. Budgeting is not just a financial or political activity, but is also a planning/analytical activity "involving analyses and judgments about the worth of things."[5] Budgeteers use a wide selection of planning and analytical tools including: cost-benefit analysis, cost-effectiveness analysis, net present value analysis, multiple regression analysis, fiscal impact analysis, weighting and scoring techniques, strategic planning, performance measurement, program evaluation, and activity-based costing. These tools can be used for taxation decisions, resource allocation decisions, and to make government more efficient and effective.

The purpose of budgeting in its planning/analytical aspect is to make the most effective and efficient use of government resources. The budget process should incorporate a long-term perspective, establish linkages to broad organizational goals, focus budget decisions on results and outcomes, and provide incentives to government management and employees.[6]

Administrative Aspect. A chief role of the budget office is that of a coordinator. The budget office integrates the top-down plans from the chief executive and the bottom-up requests from departments. Even in governments in which the budget office (or budget personnel) has only a limited role, it will still act as a coordinator—developing the budget calendar, coordinating meetings, developing and reviewing forms and worksheets, and assisting the chief executive to prepare the budget document. After a budget is adopted, the budget office controls the apportionment and allotment of government funds. Administratively, the purpose of budgeting is to effectively coordinate the preparation of the budget and to control the apportionment and allotment of government funds to ensure that they are spent in accordance with the approved budget.

Communicative Aspect. The budget office plays the role of a communications hub (see Exhibit 1-2). It receives goals and priorities from the government's elected leadership and translates these into budget instructions for operating departments, and eventually, a proposed budget. Further into the process, it receives budget requests from de-

Exhibit 1-2 ■ The Budget Office as a Communications Hub

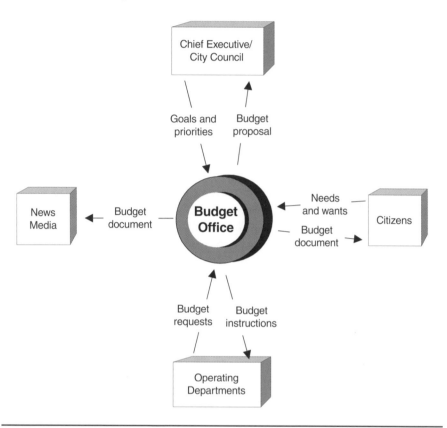

partments and converts these into a format (e.g., line item budget, program budget, performance budget, etc.) that helps decision makers to make informed choices. Throughout the process it receives input from residents and businesses. After a budget is adopted, the budget office packages the budget document in a clear, easy-to-use format for citizens and the news media. In its communicative aspect, the purpose of budgeting is to "help decision makers make informed choices about the provision of services and capital assets and to promote stakeholder participation in the process."[7]

ORGANIZATION OF THE BOOK

This book covers the functions, organizational structure, and staffing of the budget office in state and local governments. Following the introduction, Chapter 2 discusses the activities that budget offices typically perform. This discussion includes core budgeting activities, such as coordinating the budget process, as well as activities that are closely related to budgeting, such as grant management, debt issuance, and program evaluation.

Chapter 3 discusses the placement of the budget office in the government organization and the organizational structure within the budget office itself. This chapter addresses the issue of whether the budget office should report directly to the chief financial officer or the chief executive.

Chapter 4 focuses on the staffing of the budget office. This chapter shows how the dramatic changes in public budgeting in the past forty years have changed the type of work that is performed by budget office staff. This chapter includes five strategies for coordinating budget office staff and several benchmarks for the number of budget staff in states and large local governments.

Finally, Chapter 5 shows how to implement four NACSLB budgeting practices that are related to the organization of the budget office and the coordination of the budget process.

NACSLB'S RECOMMENDED PRACTICES ON COORDINATING THE BUDGET PROCESS

This book shows how to implement four recommended practices in element 8 of the NACSLB budgeting framework. Element 8 focuses on the administrative structure and coordination necessary to have an effective budget process. Readers will find helpful guidance and examples that illustrate the following budget practices:

- **Practice 8.1—Develop a budget calendar**
  A government should publish a comprehensive budget calendar that specifies when budget tasks are to be completed and that identifies timelines for those tasks.

- **Practice 8.2—Develop budget guidelines and instructions**
  A government should prepare general guidelines and budget preparation instructions for each budget cycle.

- **Practice 8.3—Develop mechanisms for coordinating budget preparation and review**
  A government should develop mechanisms and assign responsi-

bilities to provide for overall coordination of the preparation and review of the budget.

- **Practice 8.5—Identify opportunities for stakeholder input**
  A government should provide opportunities in the budget process for obtaining stakeholder input.

Endnotes

1. Lon Sprecher views budgeting to be a "unified series of steps undertaken to link and implement four functions: policy development, financial planning, service/operations planning, and communications." Lon Sprecher, "Operating Budgets," *Local Government Finance: Concepts and Practices* (Chicago: Government Finance Officers Association, 1991), 46.
2. National Advisory Council on State and Local Budgeting (NACSLB), *Recommended Budget Practices: A Framework for Improved State and Local Government Budgeting* (Chicago: Government Finance Officers Association, 1998), 3.
3. Distinguished Budget Presentation Awards Program: Awards Criteria (Chicago: Government Finance Officers Association, August 1993).
4. Robert L. Bland and Irene S. Rubin, *Budgeting: A Guide for Local Governments* (Washington, D.C.: International City/County Management Association, 1997), 11-19.
5. Edward Lehan, *Simplified Governmental Budgeting* (Chicago: Government Finance Officers Association, 1981), vi.
6. The NACSLB identifies these as four of the five essential features of a good budget process. NACSLB, *Recommended Budget Practices*, 3.
7. NACSLB, *Recommended Budget Practices*, 3.

CHAPTER 2

The Functions of the Budget Office

This chapter examines the question, *What responsibilities should be given to the budget office?* Budget offices can have a very limited role or a very broad role encompassing many activities closely related to budgeting. At one end of the spectrum, the budget office acts simply as a coordinator of the budget process, keeping the process on schedule, designing standard forms, and verifying the accuracy and completeness of budget requests. At the other end of the spectrum, the budget office not only has a larger role in the budget—evaluating department requests, balancing revenues and expenditures, and monitoring the implementation of the budget—but also takes on activities that are closely related to budgeting, such as capital planning, grant management, program evaluation, and debt analysis.

CORE BUDGETING ACTIVITIES

The core activity of the budget office is to prepare the operating budget and oversee its implementation. The most basic role that a budget office may have is that of a coordinator of the budget process. When acting as a coordinator, the budget unit develops the budget calendar, coordinates meetings, develops and reviews forms and worksheets, and assists the chief executive to prepare the budget document (National Advisory Council on State and Local Budgeting (NACSLB) practices 8.1, 8.2, 8.3, 8.4, 8.5).

In addition to coordinating the budget process, the budget office may also perform significant analytical and policy guidance functions such as evaluating department requests, balancing revenues and expenditures, and making recommendations to the chief executive (9.5).[1] In this larger role, the budget office helps to shape the *substance* of the budget (i.e., policies and programs), not just the *process* of the budget.

After a budget has been adopted, the budget office may also be given the responsibility to supervise the implementation of the budget. In this role, the budget office monitors departmental spending, reviews budget transfer requests (12.1), and generates regular, mid-year budget reports (11.2). Exhibit 2-1 lists the specific activities for each of these three roles of coordination, policy guidance, and implementation.

There are a number of advantages to giving the budget office a broad set of core responsibilities including responsibility for coordination, policy guidance, and supervision. Some of these advantages are:

1. Competing priorities for services can best be determined from a central vantage point;

2. Budget preparation is facilitated through standardized procedures and forms;

3. Effective control of local government resources can be achieved more easily since the in- and outflow of these resources is handled through one official (or one organizational unit). Control through a single official can also improve internal controls and minimize employee risk factors;

4. Fiscal problems can be detected sooner because dedicated staff with budgetary and financial experience review departments' service levels in a timely manner;

5. Budget implementation is facilitated by the use of standard forms for all budget actions, such as submitting requests for transfer of funds, new positions, or changes in existing positions; and,

6. A central budget office can help to "level the playing field" between departments, so that a more politically connected department cannot so easily do an end run to the CEO at the expense of other departments.[3]

Exhibit 2-1 ■ Core Activities of the Budget Office[2]

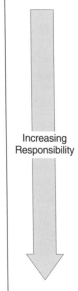

Increasing Responsibility

Coordination

1. Develops budget calendar or schedule.
2. Designs budget worksheets and forms.
3. Assists departments to formalize performance measures (if applicable).
4. Develops budget worksheet instructions for department heads.
5. Reviews finished worksheets for accuracy and completeness.
6. Prepares or assembles revenue estimates.
7. Presents budgetary materials to chief executive for review.
8. Assists chief executive official to prepare recommended budget for elected officials.
9. Coordinates activities and schedules meetings.

Policy Guidance

1. Issues guidelines to departmental officials regarding acceptable levels of service increases or decreases and expected cost limitations.
2. Evaluates departmental requests and adjusts them to policy guidelines.
3. Develops budget objectives of the locality including any constraints which may be imposed.
4. Ensures consistency of requests within and among departments.
5. Balances expenditure request with available revenues.
6. Makes recommendations for budget action to legislative body.

Supervision of Budget Implementation

1. Ensures that departments do not exceed budget limits by conducting periodic projections of expenditures and comparing them to available resources.
2. Reviews all requests to transfer from one budget item to another.
3. Maintains and updates manual of budget procedures.
4. Prepares reports on budgetary performance for the use of legislative body, chief executive, and departments.
5. Closely monitors departmental performance to determine potential adverse trends.

ACTIVITIES RELATED TO BUDGETING

In addition to the core activity of preparing and implementing the operating budget, the budget office may also be given the responsibility for other activities closely related to budgeting. For example, a budget office may be given responsibility for revenue forecasting and long-term financial planning because these activities provide key information that is necessary to prepare the operating budget. A budget office also may be given responsibility for employee position control and capital budgeting because these activities have a major effect on a budget office's ability to balance the operating budget. Program evaluation and performance measurement activities may also be assigned to the budget office

Exhibit 2-2 ■ Activities Closely Related to the Preparation and Control of the Operating Budget

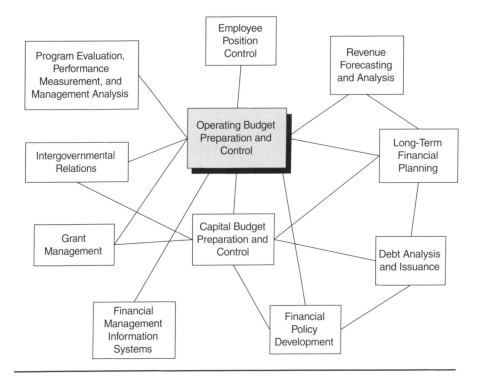

because they enable it to oversee the implementation of the operating budget in a more complete way. Exhibit 2-2 shows the interrelationships between the preparation and control of the operating budget and ten other activities.

There are two fundamentally different visions among practitioners regarding the scope and responsibilities of the budget office. In one vision, the budget office is a "satellite" of the finance department or administration department. In this vision, providing financial or administrative services is the focus and the budget unit is merely a supporting player. Here, the budget office has a narrowly defined role.

In the second vision, the budget office is the focus. In this vision, all activities related to budgeting, such as debt issuance and performance measurement, are "satellites" of the budget function, and the budget office has a broadly defined role. In actual practice, most governments may have some combination of these two visions. This section will examine the functions of the budget office from the point of view of the second vision in which the budget office is given responsibility for (or at least plays a key role in) activities closely related to budgeting.[4]

The challenge in assigning responsibilities to the budget office is that many activities that are closely related to budgeting are also related to other government functions. For example, the capital budget is closely related to the operating budget, so a convincing argument can be made that this responsibility should be located in the budget office. However, the capital budget is also a tool of long-term planning, so it might also be located in the planning department. Alternatively, it might also be located in the public works department because it has a major effect on infrastructure. Another example is employee position control. Since personnel expenditures are typically the largest portion of the operating budget, one might argue that the budget office should have control over the number of employee positions in the government. However, position control is also a human resource issue and might also be located in the personnel department.

Technological advances may, to some extent, solve this dilemma. Innovations such as network computing, electronic mail, and enterprise resource planning systems enable coordination between employees that previously was only practical between individuals in the same department. Future advancements in information technology may enable government employees to both remain in specialized units and coordinate on tasks related to several departments. This alternative type of organizational structure is known as a matrix organization. Exhibit 2-3 illustrates the concept of a matrix organization. In this diagram, departments are represented by columns and activities by rows. Thus, the capital budgeting activity in the second row includes three employees from Budget, two employees from Planning, and one employee from the Public Works Department. Thus, an employee can be both a member of the budget department, and a member of a project team to develop the capital budget. Although the concept of a matrix organization has been around for many years, it has become more practical due to advances in technology.

Exhibit 2-2 showed that the operating budget is closely related to ten other activities. The following sections will define each of these activities and discuss how they are related to the operating budget.

Exhibit 2-3 ■ A Matrix Organization

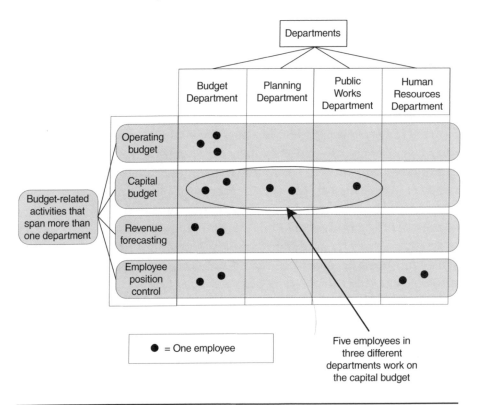

NACSLB practices that are related to each function are noted with their identification number in parentheses.

Operating Budget Preparation. Preparing the operating budget includes producing the written budget document and coordinating the development, discussion, and adoption of the budget. Fifteen NACSLB practices are related to this function.

Coordinating the development of the budget involves: producing a budget calendar, identifying responsibilities for completing various tasks, ensuring that various parts of the budget process are properly integrated, keeping the process on schedule, producing reports, identifying issues and problems, and ensuring that other requirements are met and quality standards are maintained (7.3, 8.3, 8.1). The development of the budget also includes issuing budget policy guidelines and budget preparation instructions. Budget policy guidelines set forth financial constraints and key assumptions that will be used to guide the development of the budget. Budget preparation instructions are based on these policy guidelines and often include sample forms to be completed by operating departments or program heads (8.2). Coordinating the discussion of the budget includes providing opportunities in the budget process for obtaining stakeholder input such as public hearings and opinion surveys (8.5). Prior to making decisions about specific programs and revenue sources, the budget office should first consider the "big picture" of how total revenue and expenditure levels will affect the government's financial condition in the budget period and future years (9.5).

Another major responsibility of the budget office is to review and integrate departmental budget requests and generate a proposed budget for the chief executive or governing body. The written budget document is a set of recommended actions regarding programs and services to be funded, including service level, quality, and goals to be achieved. It identifies funding requirements and sources of funds, and provides the supplemental information necessary to comprehend and review the plans (10.1). The budget should be presented in a clear and readily comprehensible format. Some items in a budget document that will assist the reader include: a table of contents, summaries, a consistent format, high-level summary information that describes overall funding sources and the organization as a whole, and charts and graphs to better illustrate important points (10.1g). The NACSLB recommends that governments include the following items in the budget document:

- A description of key programmatic and financial policies, plans, and goals (10.1a)
- An identification and analysis of key issues and major programmatic and financial changes (10.1b)
- A financial overview—A description of the short- and long-term financial plan of the government (10.1c)
- A guide to operations—Information that provides the reader with a guide to the programs the government operates and the organizational structure in place to provide those programs and services (10.1d)
- An explanation of the budgetary basis of accounting—A description of the relationship between the form of accounting used to describe revenues and expenditures in the budget, and

the form of accounting used to prepare the annual financial report (10.1e)

- A budget summary—A summary of both the proposed and final
budget (10.1f).[5]

Coordinating the adoption of the budget by the legislative body involves developing processes to facilitate its review. Some examples of
these processes include: small group meetings, hearings, workshops,
specific decision-making techniques and procedures, conflict resolution processes, and methods for presenting portions of the budget (8.4,
10.2).

Operating Budget Control. Operating budget control includes:

- Estimating and monitoring monthly or quarterly expenditures
and revenues throughout the budget year,
- Periodic reporting of actual expenditures and revenues compared to budgeted amounts (11.2),
- Recommending mid-year adjustments to the governing body
(12.1), and
- Monitoring progress of services (12.2).

Since the information on current expenditures and revenues obtained through budget control is crucial for accurate future budget
planning, it is preferable that this activity is placed in the same unit that
develops the operating budget.

**Capital Budget and Capital Improvement Program Development
and Control.** A capital improvement program (CIP) is a multi-year plan
for capital expenditures. A capital budget is usually the first year in the
capital improvement plan. The CIP is typically a tentative plan,
whereas the capital budget is a legal appropriation. The development of
the CIP involves: developing capital project evaluating criteria (5.2),
preparing a capital needs assessment (2.2), identifying projects for the
capital program (6.2), undertaking financial capacity analysis, evaluating funding options, evaluating and programming capital projects, and
adopting and implementing the CIP (9.6).[6]

The CIP and capital budget are closely related to the operating
budget. Capital projects can generate significant ongoing, operating expenditures in addition to the initial capital expenditure. Likewise, operating expenditures can significantly affect the need for capital expenditures. For example, deferring maintenance expenses over a long period

can accelerate the need to replace infrastructure and capital equipment. In addition, fund balance and debt service levels in the operating budget determine whether capital projects are affordable.

Debt Analysis & Issuance. Debt analysis and issuance involves the planning, issuance, and administration of debt and other financing instruments. This includes:

- Developing a debt policy (4.3, 4.3a)
- Analyzing debt capacity[7]
- Planning and issuing new debt
- Administering existing debt
- Coordinating communication with credit rating agencies and investors.[8]

Since debt service obligations can have a significant long-term impact on a budget office's ability to balance the operating budget, it is preferable that the budget office be given the primary responsibility for planning debt issuance. At minimum, debt issuance should be closely coordinated with the budget office because it has the best understanding of the government's long term balance between resources and requirements.

Employee Position Control. Employee position control monitors the hiring and compensation of new employees to ensure that these activities are consistent with the approved budget and locality-wide pay plan. It may also include analysis of historical attrition savings, benefit costing, and contractual and grant staffing control. In a typical general purpose government, personnel expenditures comprise about 60 percent to 80 percent of total general fund expenditures. Since personnel expenditures are a major component of operating expenditures, it is desirable that the budget office be given control over employee positions so that it can have more control over balancing the operating budget.

Financial Management Information System. A financial management information system is a computer hardware and software system that manages the finance function's information processing needs. Because of the budget office's critical need for sophisticated analytical capability and up-to-date information, it is important that the budget office play a key role in the selection and use of a financial information system. For example, the budget office requires up-to-date accounting data from the financial system to provide early warning of financial emergencies and accurately forecast future revenues and expenditures.

Financial Policy Development. Financial policies establish guidelines for a government's financial practices. Governments should develop a comprehensive set of financial policies, including policies for budgeting. The NACSLB recommends that governments develop policy regarding the following nine topics.

- Develop policy on stabilization funds (4.1)
- Develop policy on fees and charges (4.2)
- Develop policy on debt issuance and management (4.3)
- Develop policy on debt level and capacity (4.3a)
- Develop policy on use of one-time revenues (4.4)
- Evaluate the use of unpredictable revenues (4.4a)
- Develop policy on balancing the operating budget (4.5)
- Develop policy on revenue diversification (4.6)
- Develop policy on contingency planning (4.7)

Since a government's financial policies can have an important affect on the government's financial condition, the budget office should play a key role in their development.

Long-term Financial Planning. Long-term financial planning is a process that assesses the long-term financial implications of current and proposed policies, programs, and assumptions. A long-range financial plan includes: an analysis of past financial trends (11.3); long-term forecasts of future revenues and expenditures that use alternative economic, planning, and policy assumptions; and an assessment of the problems and opportunities the community will face in the future and actions needed to address these issues (9.1).

For budgeting to be really effective, it requires a longer perspective than just the upcoming fiscal year. By using long term financial planning to gain a long-term view, governments can spot long term trends and consider the future consequences of current decisions. With adequate forewarning of impending crises, governments can avoid drastic cuts in service or costly remedies. This long-term view can show a government where it can improve its fiscal health and avoid putting an unfair burden on future generations. Since the budget office is responsible for balancing the budget over the long term, it is logical that it be given responsibility for long term financial planning.

Management of Grants and Alternative Funding Sources. Grant management involves coordinating the government's grant proposals, researching opportunities to increase grant revenue, recording grant-related transactions to comply with grant regulations, and preparing financial reports for grantor agencies. In addition to grants, many governments also seek other alternative funding sources to supplement tax revenue. These alternative funding sources may include: aggressive collection programs, new fees and charges, marketing of government assets, trusts, and endowments.

Giving the responsibility for grant management and researching alternative revenue sources to the budget office has several advantages. First, since the budget office has the best overall view of the government's service and capital needs, it is able to seek grants and alternative revenues that meet the most pressing service and capital needs. Second, if the budget office has the primary responsibility for seeking grants and alternative revenues, then it will have the best understanding of the reliability of these revenues. It is also in the best position to pursue other sources of funding if grant funding is lost and meet continued program expenditures after a grant expires. Finally, the financial aspects of grant management combined with the need to coordinate activities across departments lend themselves to the budget office which plays a similar role in the development of the budget.[9]

Intergovernmental Relations. Intergovernmental relations includes the responsibility for: 1) monitoring and assessing the fiscal impact of state and federal policies and actions, 2) pursuing joint activities with other governmental entities (e.g., regional service delivery mechanisms, joint purchasing, sharing capital assets, etc.), and 3) evaluating the costs and benefits of consolidation. The budget office should play a coordinating role in intergovernmental relations because it has the best overall view of the government's short and long term financial condition and plans, and thus is best qualified to assess the fiscal impact of state and federal policies and the costs and benefits of joint activities with other governments.

Program Evaluation, Performance Measurement, and Management Analysis. This function encompasses a broad range of planning, analysis, and evaluation activities, including:

- Assessing community needs, priorities, challenges, and opportunities (1.1, 1.2);

- Identifying opportunities and challenges for government services, capital assets, and management practices (2.1, 2.2, 2.3);
- Developing and disseminating broad goals (3.1, 3.2);
- Developing programmatic, operating and capital plans (5.1, 5.2);
- Analyzing options for providing services and meeting capital needs (6.1, 6.2);
- Developing management strategies (7.1, 7.2, 7.3); and,
- Developing performance measures and benchmarks and evaluating the efficiency and effectiveness of government programs (6.4, 6.4a, 11.1, 11.1a).[10]

According to the NACSLB, a good budget process, "establishes linkages to broad organizational goals," "focuses budget decisions on results and outcomes," and "provides incentives to government management and employees."[13] For the budget to be linked to goals, focused on results, and provide incentives, it is preferable that the budget office be the focal point for goal setting, performance measurement, and management analysis.[12]

Revenue and Expenditure Forecasting and Analysis. Revenue forecasting is the process of estimating or projecting future revenues and other resources using quantitative or qualitative techniques (9.2). This may include analyzing major revenue sources (9.2a), evaluating the effect of changes to revenue source rates and bases (9.2b),[13] analyzing tax and fee exemptions (9.2c), and documenting revenue sources in a revenue manual (9.3). Expenditure forecasting is the process of preparing multi-year projections of expenditures (9.4).[14]

Since revenue and expenditure forecasting are integral parts of the operating budget, it is preferable that they be included in the budget office. Revenue forecasting shows the amount of resources that are available for the budget, while expenditure forecasting shows the amount of requirements. In addition, since the budget office is responsible for balancing the budget over the long term, it is also preferable that it have a significant role in analyzing and setting rates and fees so that it can influence future revenue streams.

CURRENT PRACTICE

Few large-scale studies exist on the responsibilities given to budget offices in actual practice. The following paragraphs summarize the find-

Exhibit 2-4 ■ The Combined Results of Three Studies of Budget Office Responsibilities

Budget Office Responsibility	All Local Governments[15]	Large City and County Governments[16]	State Governments[17]
Revenue forecasting	92%	100%	73%
Preparing proposed budget	99%	100%	(no data)
Monitoring department expenditures	89%	100%	(no data)
Monitoring department performance/ program evaluation	69%	90%	88%
Debt management	(no data)	40%	43%

ings of four studies of state and local government budget offices. Although the studies asked different sets of questions and focused on different types of governments, Exhibit 2-4 attempts to combine the results of three of these studies.

Exhibit 2-4 shows that most budget offices in local governments (89 percent to 100 percent) are responsible for revenue forecasting, preparing the proposed budget, and monitoring department expenditures. Revenue forecasting is somewhat less prevalent in state budget offices (73 percent) than in local government budget offices (92 percent to 100 percent). Most state and local government budget offices (69 percent to 90 percent) are responsible for monitoring the performance of operating departments or performing program evaluations. Debt management responsibilities are less frequently given to budget offices. About 40 percent of the budget offices in *large* city and county governments and state governments have responsibility for debt management.

Local Governments. A survey of budget offices in 510 local governments showed that most budget offices have responsibility for revenue estimation, budget preparation, and budget monitoring. A smaller percentage conduct performance audits. Exhibit 2-5 presents the survey results.

Another survey of 551 local governments, conducted by the Government Finance Officers Association, showed that the budgeting function tends to be highly correlated with the analysis and research activity. Budgeting is also moderately correlated with debt issuance and administra-

Exhibit 2-5 ■ Budget Office Responsibilities in Local Governments[18]

Budget Responsibility	Percent of Budget Offices with Responsibility
Packaging proposed budget	99%
Analyzing department requests	93%
Formulating revenue estimates	92%
Monitoring department expenditures	89%
Making allocation recommendations	88%
Monitoring department performance	69%
Conducting performance audits	19%

Exhibit 2-6 ■ Correlation Between Budgeting and Other Related Finance Activities[19]

Related Finance Activity	Correlation with Budgeting
Analysis & Research	0.4757
Debt Issuance	0.3451
Debt Administration	0.3046
Central Accounting	0.2964
Grants Management	0.2777

tion. The correlations in Exhibit 2-6 show the extent to which related finance activities are under the same finance official responsible for budgeting. In other words, the correlation can show whether related finance activities tend to be placed in a budget office. A correlation of 1.0 means that an activity is always placed in the same office with the budgeting function. A correlation of –1.0 means that an activity is never placed in the same office with budgeting. Exhibit 2-6 shows five major finance activities that had the highest correlation with the budgeting function.

Large City and County Governments. The survey of 510 local governments found that among large governments the budget office was more likely to monitor the performance of operating departments. Jurisdictions with a population greater than 250,000 were more likely to monitor departments' performance than smaller jurisdictions, and jurisdictions with a population greater than 50,000 were more likely to conduct performance audits.

Exhibit 2-7 ■ Percentage of Budget Offices with Specific Functional Responsibilities[20]

Area	Responsibility	Percentage with Full Responsibility	Percentage with Full or Partial Responsibility
Financial Planning	Develops the government's financial policies	60%	80%
	Prepares forecasts of revenues and expenditures	90%	100%
	Prepares multi-year financial plans	70%	80%
Capital and Debt	Prepares capital budget/CIP	80%	90%
	Monitors capital budget	90%	90%
	Debt management	40%	40%
Budget Preparation & Control	Prepares budget guidelines and instructions	90%	100%
	Prepares proposed budget	90%	100%
	Monitors departmental budget execution	100%	100%
	Controls employee positions	70%	80%
	Recommends mid-year budget adjustments	90%	90%
Program Evaluation & Management Analysis	Develops performance measures and benchmarks	60%	90%
	Evaluates the efficiency and effectiveness of programs and units	60%	90%
Employee Relations	Labor negotiations; compensation plan	30%	90%
	Monitors performance of employees in operating departments	30%	40%
Grant Management	Coordinates and seeks state/federal grants/funding	30%	40%
	Grant administration	40%	60%

A GFOA Research & Consulting Center study of ten large city and county governments found that budget offices in these governments perform many of the same activities. Exhibit 2-7 lists traditional budget office activities and the percentage of budget offices with responsibility for each activity.

Exhibit 2-7 shows that nearly all (90 percent to 100 percent) of the budget offices in the sample have full or partial responsibility for performing the following responsibilities:

- Prepares forecasts of revenues and expenditures;
- Prepares capital budget/CIP;
- Monitors capital budget;
- Prepares budget guidelines and instructions;
- Prepares proposed budget;
- Monitors departmental budget execution;
- Recommends mid-year budget adjustments;
- Develop performance measures and benchmarks;
- Evaluates the efficiency and effectiveness of programs and unit; and,
- Labor negotiations; compensation plan;

In addition to carrying out the above responsibilities, most (more than 60 percent) budget offices perform the following responsibilities:

- Develops financial policies;
- Prepare multi-year financial plans;
- Controls employee positions; and,
- Grant administration.

Relatively few budget offices monitor the performance of employees in operating departments and few are responsible for debt management. In terms of overall span of control, the average government in this sample had full responsibility for eleven functions, partial responsibility for two functions, and no responsibility for four of the seventeen functions listed in Exhibit 2-7.

State Governments. A study of budget offices in the fifty U.S. states and Puerto Rico conducted by the National Association of State Budget Officers found that 88 percent to 98 percent of budget offices are responsible for reviewing legislation, management analysis, and program evaluation (see Exhibit 2-8). Most budget offices (71 percent to 80 percent) are also responsible for fiscal notes, planning, revenue estimating, and economic analysis. Some state budget offices (29 percent to 41 percent) also have non budget-related responsibilities such as cash management, accounting, and pre-audit.

Exhibit 2-8 ■ State Government Budget Agency Functions[21]

Responsibility	Percent of States
Review Legislation	98%
Management Analysis	90%
Program Evaluation	88%
Fiscal notes	80%
Planning	80%
Revenue Estimating	73%
Economic Analysis	71%
Debt Management	43%
Demographic Analysis	43%
Cash Management	41%
Contract Approval	39%
Data Processing	39%
Accounting	33%
Pre-Audit	29%
Tax Expenditure Report Preparation	25%

SUMMARY

This chapter discussed the issue of what responsibilities should be given to the budget office. The most narrow role of the budget office is simply a coordinator of the budget process. Some governments give the budget office broader responsibilities of policy guidance and monitoring the implementation of the budget. In its broadest role, the budget office also has responsibility for activities closely related to budgeting such as debt issuance and program evaluation. The current practice among local governments of all sizes is to give the budget office responsibility for revenue forecasting, preparing the proposed budget, and monitoring department expenditures. A majority of governments also give the budget office responsibility for monitoring the performance of operating departments. The next chapter will examine the placement of the budget office in the government organization and the organizational structure within the budget office.

Endnotes

1. Hereafter, related NACSLB budget practices are noted with their number in parentheses.
2. Adapted from Juliet Carol Powdar, *The Operating Budget: A Guide for Smaller Governments* (Chicago: Government Finance Officers Association, 1996), 9-11.
3. Much of this list is based on Powdar, 11.
4. The reader should note that there is no conclusive answer to the proper functions of the budget office and the views expressed here are not necessarily those of the GFOA or NACSLB.
5. A related GFOA Recommended Practice is "Providing a Concise Summary of the Budget (1996)."
6. Patricia Tigue, *Capital Improvement Programming: A Guide for Smaller Governments* (Chicago: Government Finance Officers Association, 1996), 7.
7. A related GFOA Recommended Practice is "Analyzing Debt Capacity and Establishing Debt Limits (1995)."
8. A related GFOA Recommended Practice is "Maintaining an Investor Relations Program (1996)."
9. As subject matter experts, operating departments should play an important role in writing grant proposals.
10. A related GFOA Recommended Practice is "Performance Measures (1994)."
11. NACSLB, 3. The NACSLB also lists two other essential features of a good budget process: "incorporates and long-term perspective," and "involves and promotes effective communication with stakeholders."
12. The government finance profession has not yet arrived at a consensus on the location of the performance measurement activity. The Governmental Accounting Standards Board (GASB) has proposed that financial and nonfinancial performance measures be included in the comprehensive annual financial report (GASB Concepts Statement No. 2, *Service Efforts and Accomplishments Reporting*, 1994). Some anticipate that this would make performance measurement primarily a financial reporting activity. The position of the GFOA is that performance measures fall within the purview of budgetary practice rather than financial reporting (GFOA Policy Statement on Service Efforts and Accomplishments, 1993).
13. A related GFOA Recommended Practice is "Setting of Government Charges and Fees (1996)."
14. A related GFOA Recommended Practice is "Financial Forecasting in the Budget Preparation Process (1999)."
15. Sample: 510 U.S. local government jurisdictions drawn from the active GFOA membership. Source: Daniel E. O'Toole, James Marshall, and Timothy Grewe, "Current Local Government Budgeting Practices," *Government Finance Review* (December 1996): 25-29.
16. Sample: Ten large U.S. city and county governments. The ten governments included in this survey were: City of New York, New York; City of Chicago, Illinois; City of Phoenix, Arizona; Los Angeles County, California; Fairfax County, Virginia; City of San Diego, California; City of Portland, Oregon; City of Los Angeles, California; City of Philadelphia, Pennsylvania; and District of Columbia. The percentages here are the percent of the sample with full or partial responsibility for these functions. Source: GFOA Research and Consulting Center survey, August 2000.
17. Sample: Budget offices in the 50 U.S. states and Puerto Rico. Source: *Budget Processes in the States* (National Association of State Budget Officers, October 1999), 6-9.
18. O'Toole, et al.
19. Sample: 1,317 chief finance officials in 551 government jurisdictions within the United States and Canada. Source: John E. Petersen, Pat Watt, and Paul Zorn, *Organization and Compensation in Local Government Finance* (Chicago: Government Finance Officers Association, 1986), 56-57.
20. GFOA Research and Consulting Center survey.
21. NASBO, 6-9.

The Organizational Structure of the Budget Office

This chapter begins by discussing four major ways of placing the budget office in the larger government organization. The placement of the budget office raises the important issue of whether it should report directly to the Chief Financial Officer or the Chief Executive. The chapter addresses this issue and reports on the current practice among local governments for placing the budget office within their organizations. Following this, the discussion "zooms in" to look at the organizational structure *within* the budget office.

THE LOCATION OF THE BUDGET OFFICE IN THE GOVERNMENT ORGANIZATION

State and local governments generally place the budget office in one of four locations:

- As a freestanding department;
- Inside the chief executive's or top manager's office;
- Inside the finance department; or,
- Inside an administration department.

The following paragraphs discuss each of these structures and report their prevalence in state and local governments.

Freestanding Budget Office. A freestanding budget office has departmental status and reports directly to the chief executive, as opposed to being a subunit of another government department. Two prominent examples of freestanding budget offices are the Offices of Management and Budget in the Cities of Chicago and New York. Both of these budget offices have traditional budget office responsibilities of preparing and monitoring the operating and capital budgets and evaluating government programs. A variation of the freestanding budget office is a freestanding office that reports to a *deputy* chief executive. One example is the Budget and Research Office in the City of Phoenix, whose budget director reports to a deputy city manager (see Exhibit 3-1). (The finance director reports to a different deputy city manager.)

Freestanding budget offices are more prevalent in larger governments.[1] Research by the Government Finance Officers Association (GFOA) on chief finance officials found that only 1 to 4 percent of smaller governments[2] have a Budget Director. This percentage jumps to 27 percent for governments with a population of 100,000–500,000, and to 40 percent for governments with a population greater than 500,000 (see Exhibit 3-2).[3] The existence of a Budget Director who does not report to another chief finance official suggests that a government has either a freestanding budget office or a budget office in the chief executive's office.

Budget Office within the Chief Executive's Office. Placing the budget office within the chief executive's office makes the budget office a subunit of the mayor or city manager's office. This placement gives the budget office a closer relationship to the chief executive and gives the chief executive more direct control over budgeting activities. Being located in the chief executive's office may also increase the policy/political orientation of the budget office. Two examples of governments with this type of budget office are the City of Riverside, California (with a budget office in the City Manager's Office) and the County of Alameda, California (with a budget office in the County Administrator's Office).

Budget Office Inside the Finance Department. Many governments place the budget function inside a finance department with other finance activities. In this arrangement, the budget function is treated like any other finance activity such as central accounting, disburse-

Exhibit 3-1 ■ A Freestanding Budget Office
City of Phoenix, Arizona—Budget and Research Department

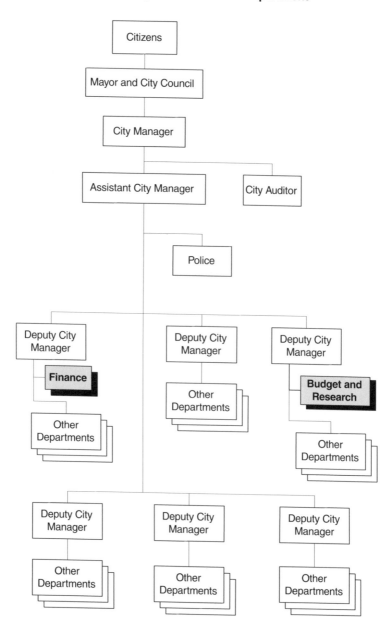

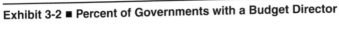

Exhibit 3-2 ■ Percent of Governments with a Budget Director

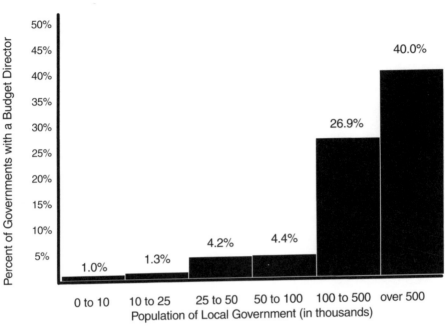

ments, and treasury management. The chief budget officer may be either the finance director or the head of the budget unit who reports to the finance director.

Locating the budget function in the finance office may tend to insulate it from politics and policy-making and increase its technical orientation. Governments may also place the budget office inside the finance department to increase the coordination among finance activities or simply because the size of the government does not warrant a separate budget office. In fact, governments with a population less than 50,000 usually place the budget function in the finance department.[4] Two examples of governments that place the budget function inside the finance department are the City of Baltimore's Finance Department and the City of St. Paul's Financial Services Office (see Exhibit 3-4).

One variation of placing the budget function inside the finance department is to cluster the budget unit with other finance units. Larger governments may adopt this structure because their budget unit has departmental status. A chief financial officer or secretary of finance usu-

**Exhibit 3-3 ■ A Budget Office Within the Chief Executive's Office
City of Riverside, California—City Manager's Office**

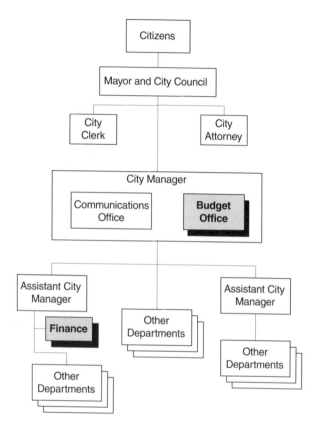

ally heads this budget and finance cluster. The Commonwealth of Virginia and Fairfax County, Virginia are two examples of governments with clusters of finance and budget offices. Exhibit 3-5 shows the subunits in both of these budget and finance clusters.

Budget Office Inside an Administration Department. An arrangement similar to locating the budget function in a finance department is to place it in a general administration department. Typically, administration departments have names such as "Administrative Services" or "Finance and Administration" and have responsibilities like treasury management, accounting, risk management, information technology, human resources, purchasing, and fleet management. In this arrangement, the budget officer typically reports to a chief adminis-

Exhibit 3-4 ■ A Budget Office Inside the Finance Office
City of Saint Paul, Minnesota Financial Services Office

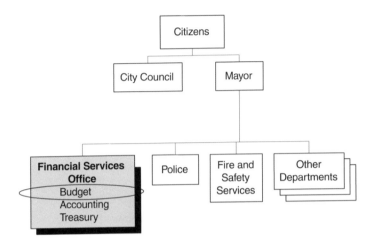

Exhibit 3-5 ■ Budget and Finance Cluster

Government	Cluster	Subunits (operating budget unit in bold)
Commonwealth of Virginia	Secretary of Finance	• **Department of Planning & Budget** • Department of Accounts • Department of Taxation • Department of Treasury • Department of the State Internal Auditor
Fairfax County	Chief Financial Officer	• **Department of Management & Budget** • Department of Finance • Department of Tax Administration • Department of Purchasing & Supply Management

trative officer. Being located in an administration department tends to give the budget office more of an administrative role and less of a policy or political role.[5] Two examples of governments that place the budget function in an administration department are the City of Jacksonville's Department of Administration and Finance (Exhibit 3-6) and the City of Milwaukee's Department of Administration.

Other Structures. Some governments do not fall exactly into a single category. For example, the City of Los Angeles has both a freestanding budget office and a Budget Director inside the mayor's office. In an

**Exhibit 3-6 ■ Budget Office inside Administration Department
City of Jacksonville, Florida—Department of Administration and Finance**

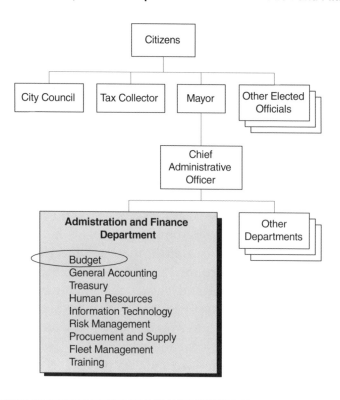

unusual structure, the City's freestanding budget office, known as the City Administrative Officer, reports both to the mayor and the city council. This arrangement has led to a situation where the mayor has a separate budget staff within his office because he does not have complete authority over the City Administrative Officer. In addition, the City Controller (an independently elected official) prepares a revenue forecast.

The City of San Francisco splits typical budget office responsibilities into two offices in different parts of the government. The Office of Budget and Legislative Affairs (in the mayor's office) and the Management, Analysis and Reports (in the Controller's Office) both have budget preparation responsibilities.

In the City of Atlanta, budget development and budget control are split between two offices within a cluster of budget and finance offices.

An office of Accounting and Budget Administration is responsible for budget control, while an office of Budget and Management Analysis is responsible for budget preparation and policy analysis. A Chief Financial Officer heads the budget and finance cluster.

The City of New Orleans splits budget responsibilities between the executive and legislative branches. The City Council has a Council Fiscal Office with a budget and research staff responsible for analyzing department budget requests, analyzing the mayor's proposed budget, and monitoring departmental operations. In the executive branch, the Finance Office has a budget unit responsible for preparing the mayor's proposed budget and monitoring the adopted budget.

Budget Offices in the Legislative Branch. The preceding paragraphs have discussed four basic methods of locating the budget office in the executive branch. However, some governments also have a significant number of budget office staff in the *legislative* branch. These staff typically report to the city council and are intended to balance budget power between the executive and legislative branches by giving legislators the analysis and fiscal expertise to question the budget proposals of the chief executive. Legislative budget offices are most prevalent in state governments and large local governments.

Federal. A prominent example of a legislative budget office on the national level is the Congressional Budget Office (CBO). The CBO provides technical research and analysis on budget and economic decisions. In addition to the CBO, two other congressional agencies have some responsibilities typically given to a budget office. The Congressional Research Service provides research and analysis on any public policy issue facing the Congress. The Government Accounting Office conducts performance audits and program evaluations.

State. Typically, state legislative budget offices have responsibility for reviewing the executive budget proposal, writing fiscal notes,[6] conducting policy analyses, and making revenue forecasts. Two examples of legislative budget offices are the State of California Legislative Analyst's Office and the State of Ohio Legislative Budget Office. The California Legislative Analyst's Office has a staff of 49. It has a broad set of responsibilities including: reviewing the Governor's proposed budget, evaluating the efficiency and effectiveness of state programs, reviewing mid-year budget adjustments, and serving as a staff resource for state legislators. The Ohio Legislative Budget Office has a staff of about 45. It is responsible for evaluating the Governor's proposed budget, writing fiscal notes, and providing fiscal and policy research for state legislators.

Local. Several examples of legislative budget offices on the local level are the cities of Baton Rouge, New Orleans, Los Angeles, San Francisco, and New York. The City of Baton Rouge's Council Budget Office has a small staff and is responsible for reviewing grants as well as providing financial research and analysis. The City of New Orleans has a Council Fiscal Office responsible for analyzing department budget requests, analyzing the mayor's proposed budget, and monitoring departmental operations. The City of Los Angeles city council has an Office of the Chief Legislative Analyst that is patterned after the California Legislative Analyst's Office. The City and County of San Francisco's Board of Supervisors has an Office of the Budget Analyst which reviews the Mayor's proposed budget and performs management audits of government departments. The City of New York has an Independent Budget Office that provides budgetary, economic, and policy analysis to both elected officials and the citizens of the city.

UNDER THE CFO OR THE CHIEF EXECUTIVE?

A major issue in the placement of the budget office is whether it should report directly to the chief financial officer (CFO) or to the chief executive. In the first alternative, the budget office may be located in a finance department, a department of finance and administration, or in a cluster of finance offices under a CFO. In the second alternative, the budget office may be located in the mayor or city manager's office, or may be a freestanding office with a direct reporting relationship with the chief executive. The following paragraphs summarize the advantages and disadvantages of both options.[7]

Placing the Budget Office under a CFO. In this alternative, the budget office reports to a CFO who is responsible for all of the government's financial functions. The CFO, in turn, reports to the chief executive. The advantages of placing the budget office under a CFO tend to be obtained by the government as a whole, while the disadvantages tend to be felt by the budget office in particular.

Advantages. The primary advantage of placing the budget office under a CFO is increased coordination (because one person oversees all of the government's finance activities). Increased coordination can make an organization more efficient and eliminate conflicts in advice and information to policy makers. It can also lead to better planning and control. A second advantage of placing the budget office under a CFO is that it should increase the accountability of the entire finance organization. Since one individual oversees all of the government's finance activities, one individual can be held responsible for a government's financial administration. In addition, since a single CFO replaces two positions with a single position, the government should be able to hire better leadership talent because it can potentially offer candidates a higher salary with more responsibility. Finally, placing the budget office under a CFO can tend to insulate it more from elected officials. This can have advantages and disadvantages. An advantage is that the budget office is in a better position to make decisions based on technical criteria (such as a long term structural balance) rather than political criteria (such as avoiding service cuts in an election year). Insulating the budget office from elected officials can also have disadvantages, which will be mentioned below.

Disadvantages. One disadvantage of placing the budget office under a CFO is that it may lead to a fragmentation of power between the chief executive and the CFO where both have responsibility for budget formulation. Because budgeting has a large political/policy-making component, the chief executive will likely have a significant role in the budgeting process. If a budget office is under a CFO, it may in practice have two bosses: the chief executive and the CFO. Another disadvantage is that if the budget office is a subunit of a larger finance cluster, it may be given a lower priority by the chief executive. A CFO may also give a higher priority to other finance functions under his or her authority at the expense of the budgeting function. As mentioned earlier, insulating the budget office more from elected officials (by placing it under a CFO) can also have disadvantages. The main disadvantages are that the budget office will likely have a smaller policy-making role and will tend to be less responsive to elected officials.

Placing the Budget Office under the Chief Executive. The alternative to placing the budget office under the authority of a CFO is to separate it from the rest of the finance organization and give the budget director a direct reporting relationship with the chief executive. In this arrangement the budget office may be located in the chief executive's office or may be a freestanding agency.

Advantages. One advantage to placing the budget office under the chief executive is that it allows the chief executive direct control over a government's budget because the budget director reports to him or her rather than to a CFO. Thus, the budget office is positioned to carry out the chief executive's priorities and vision. Another advantage is that the budget office may have a more active role in policy development because of its proximity to the city's chief policy-maker. This proximity to the chief executive may also help the budget office to obtain better responsiveness and cooperation from the operating departments since it is perceived to have more clout in the organization. A budget office that reports to the chief executive is also better suited to integrate decision making, priority setting, and the budget process. In addition, since the budget office has higher, departmental status and reports directly to the chief executive, the budgeting function may be given a higher priority by the chief executive than if it were a subfunction under a CFO.

Disadvantages. There are several potential disadvantages to placing the budget office under the chief executive. First, a budget office that reports directly to the chief executive may become embroiled in the day-to-day crises faced by the chief executive and lose the long-term view necessary to provide objective advice to the chief executive. Second, this type of budget office may find it difficult to develop a reputation for objectivity because it may be viewed as an extension of the chief executive. Third, staff in this type of budget office may tend to be generalists with less financial expertise than the budget office staff under a CFO. Fourth, because of the absence of a CFO over all finance functions, the budget office may have less coordination with other finance functions such as accounting and debt administration. Finally, a budget office directly under a chief executive may not receive the supervisory review that it would receive from a CFO.[8] (See Exhibit 3-7)

CURRENT PRACTICE

The location of the budget function depends on the size of the government. In general, larger governments tend to place the budget function in the chief executive's office or in a separate budget department that reports to the chief executive, while smaller governments tend to place it inside the finance office. A survey of 510 local governments found that 67% of the governments place the budget function inside a finance of-

Exhibit 3-7 ■ Under the CFO or the Chief Executive?

Reporting Relationship	Advantages	Disadvantages
Budget Office Directly Under CFO	• Should increase the coordination of a government's finance activities. • Single individual can be held accountable for financial management. • Should enable a government to hire better leadership talent.	• May lead to a fragmentation of power between the chief executive and the CFO. • Budgeting function may be given a lower priority by chief executive. • CFO may give a higher priority to other finance functions.
Budget Office Directly Under Chief Executive	• Allows a chief executive direct control over a government's budget. • Budget office may have a more active role in policy development. • Budget office may obtain better responsiveness and cooperation from operating departments. • Better suited to integrate decision making, priority setting, and the budget process. • Budgeting function may be given a higher priority by chief executive.	• May become embroiled in the day-to-day crises faced by the chief executive and lose long-term view. • May find it difficult to develop a reputation for objectivity. • Budget staff may tend to be generalists with less financial expertise. • May not receive the supervisory review that it would receive from a CFO. • Possible lack of coordination between budget officer and finance director.

fice or division of administration. The study found that most governments with a population less than 50,000 place the budget function as a subunit of the finance office. However, as a jurisdiction's size increased, the study found that the budget office was more likely to be a separate department reporting directly to the chief executive.[9]

State governments tend to give the governor more direct authority over the budget function. A survey of budget offices in the 50 states and Puerto Rico found that a majority (53 percent) of the states locate the budget function in the governor's office or in a budget department that reports directly to the governor. Exhibit 3-8 combines the results of both surveys.

Exhibit 3-9 shows an example of how the placement of the budgeting function may change over time. Note how the budgeting function in the City of Hartford, Connecticut has moved back and forth between the Finance Department and the City Manager's Office during a fifty-year period.

Exhibit 3-8 ■ **The Location of the Budget Office**

Location of Budget Function	All Local Governments[10]	State Governments[11]
Separate budget department	16%	24%
Part of the chief executive's office	14%	29%
In a unit that contains other fiscally oriented activities	54%	24%
In a division of administration	13%	24%

NAMING THE BUDGET OFFICE

The name of the budget office can be an important symbol of its role in the government. For example, "Budget and Financial Analysis" suggests that the budget office has primarily financial-related responsibilities, while "Office of Management and Budget" suggests that the budget office has both a financial role and a non-financial role overseeing the efficiency and effectiveness of government services. Furthermore, a government's decision to relocate the budget function may trigger a name change to signal a change in its power within the organization.

The issue of the name of the budget office is particularly relevant to larger governments, since they are more likely to have a separate, designated budget office. Exhibit 3-10 summarizes the names given to budget offices in 76 large U.S. cities.[12]

Exhibit 3-10 shows that the two most frequently used names are "Budget Office" and "Office of Management and Budget." About 60 percent of the cities have one of these two names (or a very similar name). A smaller percentage of cities have names like "Budget and Research" (12 percent), "Budget & Finance" (7 percent), "Financial Management Section" (5 percent), "Budget and Evaluation" (5 percent) or "Budget Management" (4 percent).

Appendix A shows the same dataset of budget offices, but categorized by their location in the government organization (e.g., freestanding budget offices, budget offices in a chief executive's office, budget offices in an administration department, and budget offices in a finance department). An analysis of the tables in Appendix A shows that, in large cities, "Office of Management and Budget" is the most frequently used name for freestanding budget offices, while "Budget Office" is the

Exhibit 3-9 ■ The History of the Budget Function in the City of Hartford, Connecticut—1947 to 2000

1947

The city approves a new charter and adopts a council-manager form of government. The new charter creates a Finance Department with a Finance Director appointed by the City Manger. Budgeting responsibilities are given to the Finance Department.

1960

The Finance Department grows to 69 positions. Budget and Research becomes a division within the Finance Department.

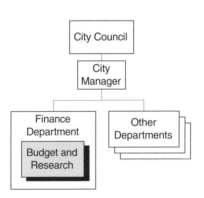

1977

Management and Budget is moved into a new Management Services Department headed by an Assistant City Manager.

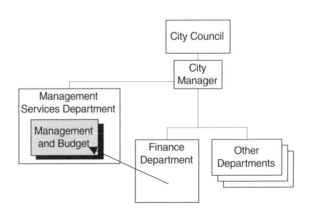

**Exhibit 3-9 ■ The History of the Budget Function
in the City of Hartford, Connecticut—1947 to 2000 (Continued)**

1987

Management and
Budget is moved back
into the Finance
Department.

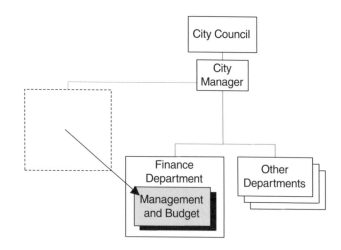

1995

Management and Budget
is moved from the
Finance Department into
the City Manager's Office.
Department-level financial
managers are moved into
the central budget office.

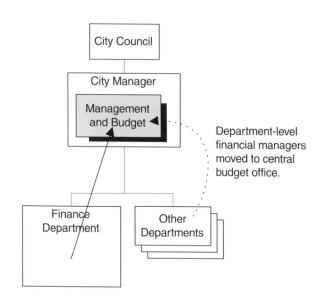

Exhibit 3-10 ■ Budget Office Names In Large Cities

Name	Number	Percent
"Budget Office" (or Budget Department; Budget Bureau; Budget Division)	26	34%
"Office of Management and Budget" (or Budget and Management Analysis; Budget and Management Division; Management Services; Administration and Budget)	20	26%
"Budget and Financial Planning" or "Budget and Research" (or Budget and Financial Analysis; Budget and Planning Division; Budget & Policy Review Division; Budget and Strategic Planning)	9	12%
"Budget and Finance Division" (or Financial Services and Budget Division; Budget and Accounting)	5	7%
"Financial Management Section" (or Financial Policy, Planning, and Analysis; Bureau of Financial Planning)	4	5%
"Budget and Evaluation" (or Bureau of Budget and Efficiency)	4	5%
"Budget Management" (or Budget Formulation and Control)	3	4%
Other	3	4%
No designated budget unit	2	3%
TOTAL	76	100%

most frequently used name for budget offices in a chief executive's office, an administration office, or a finance office.

INTERNAL BUDGET OFFICE STRUCTURE

This section examines the typical organizational structure *within* budget offices. The organizational structures of budget offices vary greatly depending on the size of the government. Small governments usually do not have a designated budget office or budget unit. In these governments, preparing the operating budget is typically a part time responsibility of the finance director or other finance department staff. Mid-sized governments are typically large enough to have designated budget divisions or budget offices. The organizational structure of these

Exhibit 3-11 ■ The Budget Office in a Small Government
City of Hurst, Texas—Fiscal Services Department

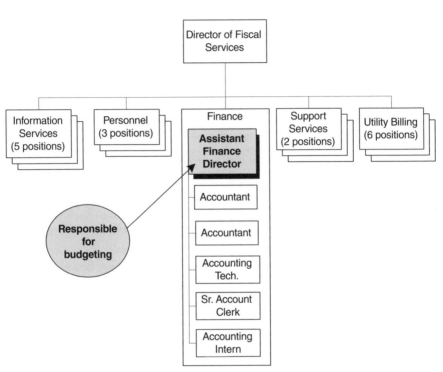

budget offices is very simple with a few employees and a single layer of hierarchy. Large governments have a more complex organizational structure, sometimes with subunits and two layers of hierarchy. Budget offices in state governments and major cities have a still more complex internal structure with highly specialized subunits.

Small Governments. Small governments are defined here as local governments with a population under 40,000 and a budget under $50 million. Governments of this size usually do not have a designated budget office or budget unit. The budget is prepared by a single person, such as the finance director, with assistance from other members of the finance department. Typically, the budget workload is not large enough to dedicate an employee full time to this activity. For example, in the City of Hurst, Texas (population 35,500), budgeting is a part-time responsibility of the Assistant Finance Director who is also responsible for internal audit, investment management, and fixed asset management. (Exhibit 3-11).

Mid-Sized Governments. Mid-sized governments are defined here as local governments with a population of 40,000 to 300,000 and a budget of $50 million to $300 million. Mid-sized governments are large enough to have designated budget divisions or budget offices. Usually, these budget offices are subunits of a finance department or a general administration department. However, in some governments they are freestanding agencies that report directly to the chief executive.

The typical budget office in a mid-sized government has a single layer of hierarchy with one budget director, two to five budget analysts, and a secretary who may be shared with another unit. The budget analysts may be of equal rank or may be organized into junior and senior analysts. In the City of Peoria, Arizona, the four budget analysts work as a team of equals and regularly rotate responsibilities among team members. In the City of Hampton, Virginia, the budget analysts are organized into senior and junior positions. Exhibit 3-12 shows the typical organizational structure of a budget office in a mid-sized government.

Budget offices are much smaller in governments with a decentralized budget process or in governments where the budget office does not evaluate department requests. Jackson County, Oregon (budget of $206 million) dedicates only two staff members to its budget part time because its budget process is decentralized. Operating departments submit complete budget packages with figures and budget narrative in an internally developed budget software system. The human resources department is responsible for position control. Typically, for a government this size, a large staff of budget analysts is needed to provide a chief executive with the information necessary to evaluate departments' requests for more funding. Jackson County reduces this need for additional analysts with two techniques that encourage operating departments to make reasonable requests for additional funding. First, departments make unresolved requests for additional funding before other department heads who can question these requests. Second, the County's internal service system charges other operating departments for particular expenditures.

The City of Springfield, Oregon (budget of $122 million) has a budget staff of about 1.5 full-time-equivalents because its budget unit has only a coordinating role and does not review department budget re-

Exhibit 3-12 ■ The Budget Office in a Mid-Sized Government
Office of Budget & Management Analysis, City of Hampton, Virginia

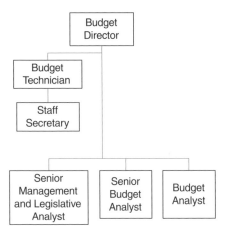

quests. Instead, this responsibility is given to an executive management team consisting of the City Manager, Assistant City Manager, Finance Director, and Budget Director.

Large Governments. Large governments are defined as cities and counties with a population of 300,000 to 900,000 and a budget of $500 million to $1 billion. Large governments typically have a budget office with about eight to fourteen positions. At this size, the organization of the budget office becomes significantly more complex. At around ten employees, budget offices typically have two layers of hierarchy with a supervisor overseeing about four to six analysts.

Some budget offices divide their staff into specialized subunits. For example, the budget office in the City of Charlotte, North Carolina has two subunits, a "Budget Development and Monitoring" unit with a budget manager and four analysts, and a "Performance Evaluation and Council Agenda" unit with three analysts and three support employees. The City of Portland's budget office, which has a staff of twelve, is organized into an Enterprise and Capital Team, a Budget Team, and a Forecast Team. Many large government budget offices have an information technology specialist such as a programmer or network technician under the budget director. Exhibit 3-14 shows the organizational structure and the assignment of responsibilities in the budget division in Pima County, Arizona. The Pima County Budget Division has a pro-

Exhibit 3-13 ■ Internal Budget Office Structures in Different Sized Governments

Government Category	Population	Operating Budget Size	Budget Office Staff	Characteristics of Budget Office
Small	Under 40,000	Under $50 million	1+	• Usually does not have a designated budget office or budget unit. • Budgeting is typically part time responsibility of finance department staff.
Mid-Sized	40,000 to 300,000	$50 to $300 million	4 to 7	• Designated budget divisions or budget offices. • One layer of hierarchy.
Large	300,000 to 900,000	$500 million to $1 billion	8 to 14	• More complex organizational structure. • Some budget offices divide their staff into subunits. • Two layers of hierarchy. • May have information technology specialist.
Very Large	Over 900,000	Over $1 billion	10 to 300	• Most budget offices subdivided into divisions.

grammer dedicated to the budget division and two layers of hierarchy with a supervisor overseeing seven analysts.

States and Major Local Governments. This final category includes state governments and local governments with a population greater than 900,000 and a budget over $1 billion. Budget offices vary in size. Some smaller state governments, such as New Hampshire and South Dakota, have small budget offices with only about ten employees. The largest state and local governments, including New York City, Los Angeles County, and New York State, have mammoth budget offices with one hundred to three hundred employees. However, the average state government has a budget office with thirty-five employees, and many major cities such as Chicago and Washington, D.C. have budget offices with about forty to fifty employees.

Due to their size, most budget offices in this category are subdivided into units or divisions. Typically, these units specialize in a particular area of budgeting, such as capital budgeting or program analysis, or specialize in a particular group of operating departments. A budget office may have anywhere from three to ten divisions, with two to fif-

Exhibit 3-14 ■ The Budget Office in a Large Government
Pima County, Arizona—Budget Division

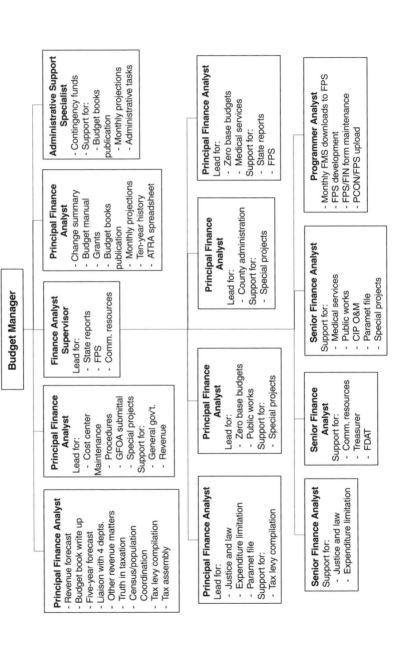

Budget Manager

Administrative Support Specialist
- Contingency funds
- Support for:
  - Budget books publication
  - Monthly projections
  - Administrative tasks

Principal Finance Analyst
- Change summary
- Budget manual
- Grants
- Budget books publication
- Monthly projections
- Ten-year history
- ATRA spreadsheet

Principal Finance Analyst
Lead for:
- Zero base budgets
- Medical services
Support for:
- State reports
- FPS

Finance Analyst Supervisor
Lead for:
- State reports
- FPS
- Comm. resources

Principal Finance Analyst
Lead for:
- County administration
Support for:
- Special projects

Programmer Analyst
- Monthly FMS downloads to FPS
- FPS development
- FPS/FIN form maintenance
- PCON/FPS upload

Principal Finance Analyst
Lead for:
- Cost center Maintenance
- Procedures
- GFOA submittal
- Special projects
Support for:
- General gov't.
- Revenue

Senior Finance Analyst
Support for:
- Medical services
- Public works
- CIP O&M
- Paramet file
- Special projects

Principal Finance Analyst
- Revenue forecast
- Budget book write up
- Five-year forecast
- Liaison with 4 depts.
- Other revenue matters
- Truth in taxation
- Census/population Coordination
- Tax levy compilation
- Tax assembly

Principal Finance Analyst
Lead for:
- Zero base budgets
- Public works
Support for:
- Special projects

Senior Finance Analyst
Support for:
- Comm. resources
- Treasurer
- FDAT

Principal Finance Analyst
Lead for:
- Justice and law
- Expenditure limitation
- Paramet file
Support for:
- Tax levy compilation

Senior Finance Analyst
Support for:
- Justice and law
- Expenditure limitation

Exhibit 3-15 ■ The Budget Office in a Major Government Commonwealth of Virginia Department of Planning & Budget

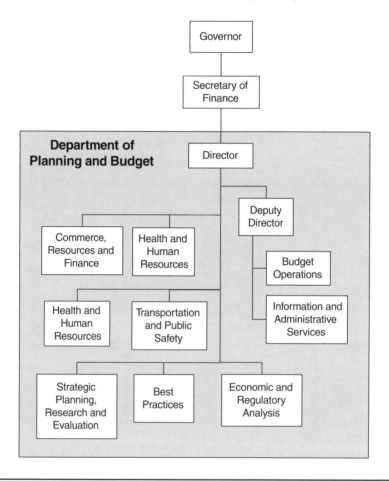

teen employees in each division. Due to its size, New York City's Office of Management and Budget (OMB) has seven large divisions, which are subdivided further into twenty-four branches. The Commonwealth of Virginia's Department of Planning & Budget has nine divisions (see Exhibit 3-15). The following paragraphs highlight several ways that states and major local governments organize the internal structure of their budget offices.

Divide into Operating or Capital Budgeting Units. Some states and major cities subdivide their budget offices into operating budget units and capital budget units. The State of Maryland Department of

Budget and Management places operating and capital budgeting in two separate offices within the department. The City of Philadelphia places operating budgeting in the Budget Bureau under the Director of Finance and capital budgeting in the Mayor's Office. Los Angeles County assigns operating and capital budget responsibilities to two separate branches within the Chief Administrative Office. Washington, D.C. organizes its budget office into five divisions, which include a capital budget, and an operating budget division.

Divide into Budgeting or Program Analysis Units. States and major cities also organize their budget offices into units that focus on budgeting and units that focus on program evaluation and management analysis. The City of Chicago's OMB has a separate Budget Development unit and Program Monitoring & Internal Audit unit. The Commonwealth of Virginia has a separate Strategic Planning, Research & Evaluation division alongside its budget analysis divisions. The State of Maryland has a separate Division of Policy Analysis within its Department of Budget and Management. The City of Los Angeles divides its City Administrative Officer's office into a Budget and Capital Programming Division and a Management Services Division (responsible for program analysis).

Divide into Units that Specialize in Particular Government Functions. Another common grouping is to organize the budget office into units that specialize in analyzing particular government agencies. The New York City's OMB has three divisions that contain nine units that specialize in analyzing particular city departments. Four of the nine divisions in Virginia's Department of Planning & Budget focus on particular broad government functions such as Education, Transportation & Public Safety, and Health & Human Resources. Fairfax County's Department of Management and Budget has five divisions that are dedicated to specific government functions. Los Angeles County's Budget and Operations Management Branch assigns three divisions with the responsibility of analyzing specific government functions.

The largest governments, such as New York City, tend to divide their budget office into units that specialize in particular government functions. While smaller governments may assign the responsibility for analyzing an agency to a single budget analyst, the size and complexity of agencies in New York City requires an entire *unit* of budget analysts.

Units with Administrative Responsibilities. Several governments give their budget offices administrative responsibilities that are related to budgeting such as employee relations, information technology, and grant management. These responsibilities are assigned to separate units within the budget offices. Two examples are the City of Chicago's OMB and the City of Los Angeles's Office of the City Administrative Officer which both have special units that monitor the productivity of city employees in operating agencies. Both cities also have special units that administer grants.

SUMMARY

State and local governments generally place the budget office in one of four locations:

1. As a freestanding department;
2. Inside the chief executive's or top manager's office;
3. Inside the finance department; or,
4. Inside an administration department.

The location of the budget office depends on the size of the government. In general, larger governments tend to place the budget function in the chief executive's office or in a separate budget department that reports to the chief executive, while smaller governments tend to place it inside the finance office. This chapter discussed the advantages and disadvantages of placing the budget office under the CFO versus the Chief Executive. Most large U.S. cities give the office with responsibility for preparing the operating budget the name "Budget Office" or "Office of Management and Budget."

The organizational structure *within* budget offices varies greatly depending on the size of the government. Small governments usually do not have a designated budget office or budget unit. In these governments, preparing the operating budget is typically a part time responsibility of the finance director or other finance department staff. Mid-sized governments are typically large enough to have designated budget divisions or budget offices. The organizational structure of these budget offices is very simple with a few employees and a single layer of hierarchy. Large governments have a more complex organizational structure, sometimes with subunits and two layers of hierarchy. Budget offices in state governments and major cities have a still more complex internal structure with highly specialized subunits. The next chapter will consider the staffing of the budget office.

Endnotes

1. Daniel E. O'Toole, James Marshall, and Timothy Grewe, "Current Local Government Budgeting Practices," *Government Finance Review* 12 (December 1996): 25-29.
2. Population less than 100,000.
3. John E. Petersen, Pat Watt, and Paul Zorn, *Organization and Compensation in Local Government Finance* (Chicago: Government Finance Officers Association, 1986), 35.
4. O'Toole et al.
5. Lon Sprecher, "Operating Budgets," *Local Government Finance: Concepts and Practices* (Chicago: Government Finance Officers Association, 1991), 50.
6. Fiscal notes are analyses that describe the effect that proposed legislation will have on state and local government revenues and expenditures.
7. The GFOA does not have a position on whether the budget office should report directly to the CFO or the chief executive. The reader should note that there is no conclusive answer to this issue and the views expressed here are not necessarily those of the GFOA or NACSLB.
8. Edward Anthony Lehan, "Organization of the Finance Function," *Local Government Finance: Concepts and Practices* (Chicago: Government Finance Officers Association, 1991), 40.
9. O'Toole et al.
10. O'Toole et al.
11. *Budget Processes in the States* (National Association of State Budget Officers, October 1999), 14-159.
12. GFOA research of seventy-six U.S. cities in 2002.

CHAPTER 4

The Staff of the Budget Office

This chapter focuses on the staffing of the budget office. Over the past few decades, a "no new taxes" political environment has created a demand for budget analysts who are not only technically proficient, but also politically savvy and creative. At the same time, technology, budgeting techniques, and education and training opportunities have changed the skill sets and type of work performed by budget analysts. The first section discusses these important changes in state and local budgeting. To help budget offices to be properly staffed to meet these changes, the second section lists the specific skills, knowledge, and abilities that a budget analyst should have for today's environment. The section that follows addresses three issues especially important in managing budget office staff: coordinating, training, and retaining staff. The chapter concludes with a discussion of the typical number of budget office staff in state governments and major local governments.

CHANGES IN STATE AND LOCAL GOVERNMENT BUDGETING

Public budgeting has undergone several dramatic changes in the past forty years. During this period, the complexity of budgeting has changed, the tools and methods of budgeting have changed, and even the types of people doing the budgeting have changed.

Effect of technology on the tools of budgeting. Not long ago, budget office staff spent much of their time retyping budget drafts, performing monotonous manual calculations, and rechecking numbers. Advances in computer hardware, network computing, spreadsheet software, and word processing software have eliminated much of the clerical work that used to be performed in the budget office. Technology has freed up analysts' time for analysis and given them sophisticated evaluative tools. However, technology has also increased expectations of what the budget office can do. For example, one veteran finance officer observed that, despite the expectation that computers would make tasks easier and employees more productive, the computer has not reduced work, but *expanded* it. Because of advances in technology, there is an expectation that finance officers can do more analysis with the numbers.[1]

Increased complexity of government services. Since World War II, local governments have experienced a dramatic expansion in the size and scope of their responsibilities. From 1957 to 1992, state and local government expenditures per capita increased 153 percent adjusted for inflation.[2] In addition, local government's scope of responsibility has expanded from police, fire, and streets to tacking complex human services issues, coordinating economic development projects, and managing cultural and recreational facilities. The increased size and scope of local government directly affects the complexity of the budgeting function. Budget staff must oversee larger budgets, more programs, and perform more complex analyses, such as evaluating private sector service providers.

"No new taxes" political environment. While the responsibilities given to governments have grown, the potential resources available to budget analysts have shrunk. Due to a change in the political climate, elected officials (and the voters they represent) are increasingly resistant to tax increases. This "no new taxes" political environment has created a demand for budget analysts who are not only technically proficient, but also politically savvy and creative. This type of budget analyst has the creativity to locate new, politically acceptable sources of revenue and to find ways of doing more with less through privatization, alternative service delivery, and increasing efficiency.

New methods of budgeting. Innovations in budgeting methods, such as program budgeting, performance budgeting, and zero-based budgeting, have changed the way that budgeting is performed. These methods alter the focus of budgeting from financial control and accountability to analyzing alternatives and achieving performance objectives. About half of local governments currently use one of these methods or a hybrid.[3]

Another important development in the past forty years has been the introduction of national guidelines for good budgeting. The Government Finance Officers Association's (GFOA) Budget Awards program sets criteria for a exemplary budget document. The National Advisory Council on State and Local Budgeting's (NACSLB) set of recommended practices provides a comprehensive set of processes and procedures that define a good budget process. Although neither of these programs are standards in the sense of being strict requirements that every government must follow, they greatly influence the sophistication and quality of local government budgeting. Moreover, they have raised the level of expectations for the quality and quantity of work put forth by budget officials.

Highly trained budget analysts. Not only have the tools, techniques, and challenges of public budgeting changed, but the skills and qualifications of budget office personnel have also changed. The introduction of graduate programs in public policy and public administration in the 1960s and 1970s has generated a pool of trained analysts. This has significantly increased the sophistication and quality of analysis that many budget offices are able to perform. For example, cost-benefit analysis, which has frequent application in budgetary work, has become a common part of graduate school curriculums.

A MODERN BUDGET ANALYST'S JOB DESCRIPTION

In many governments, budget analysts are responsible for a wide range of activities from the analysis and goal setting that occurs before the written budget document is produced, through the preparation of the budget document, to the monitoring and evaluation that occurs after the document is adopted.[4] Specifically, these responsibilities may include:

- Reviewing and evaluating budget requests;

- Projecting revenues and expenditures;
- Performing site visits to operating departments;
- Generating ideas to improve programs, find new revenues, and balance the budget;
- Helping to prepare a proposed budget document consistent with the priorities of elected leaders;
- Monitoring and analyzing accounts and budget variances;
- Approving and disapproving special expenditure requests and budget transfers;
- Performing year-end reconciliation; and,
- Producing special reports.

Personality Traits

Successful budget analysts generally possess particular personality traits. They are thorough and accurate in their work. They are creative and can generate innovative solutions. They are organized, capable of juggling many tasks, and have the ability to follow through with commitments. Finally, they have good judgement and know how to prioritize important issues from a fiscal and political/policy perspective.

Skills, Knowledge, and Abilities

This section lists the specific set of skills, knowledge, and abilities that budget analysts need in today's environment. The first category lists the specific knowledge that budget analysts need of their government's processes and finances. The next two categories list specific fundamental skills that budget analysts should possess. These fundamental skills are categorized into people/interpersonal skills and analytical skills. The last category lists specific budgeting and management innovations with which budget analysts should be familiar.[5]

Knowledge of Government's Finances and Operations. Budget analysts should have knowledge of the specific processes and financial structure of their government. They should understand their government's budget process, its accounting system, revenue and expenditure structure, and financial management system. They should also have knowledge of the operating departments that they are responsible for. Specifically, a budget analyst should possess the following:

- Understand the government's budget process and procedures outlined in its budget manual.
- Understand the government's goal-setting and policy formation process.
- Understand the government's expenditure and revenue structure and debt financing.
- Familiarity with governmental fund accounting, government's chart of accounts, and government's internal and external financial reports.
- Proficiency with government's financial management system and desktop applications.
- Knowledge of the operating departments that the analyst has responsibility over (e.g., mission, financial structure, programmatic structure, strengths, constraints, organizational structure, and personalities).
- Knowledge of the legal and regulatory impacts and constraints regarding revenues, expenditures, and the budget process.

People/Interpersonal Skills. The budget process not only includes numbers and data, but even more so includes people. Thus, budget analysts should have strong "people skills". They should understand the political environment of the budget and people's behavior in that environment. In addition, they should possess a broad array of communication skills such as interpersonal skills, persuasion skills, negotiation skills, interviewing skills, and oral and written communication skills. Specifically, a budget analyst should possess the following:

- *Interpersonal skills*—Ability to work with and develop a rapport with operating departments and program leaders. Because many of the individuals who a budget analyst contacts do not formally report to him or her, good interpersonal skills are important to obtain cooperation. Excellent networking skills are also necessary since cooperation may be required from employees across the entire organization.
- *Persuasion/marketing skills*—Ability to make a case to the chief executive, elected leaders, and oversight bodies.
- *Political savvy*—Understanding and responding appropriately to the individuals and groups with a stake in the budget;[6] understanding budget games that might be used by operating depart-

ments when obtaining funding for a new program, maintaining or increasing an existing program, or resisting budget cuts.

- *Negotiation skills*—Ability to negotiate with operating departments regarding budget requests.
- *Interviewing skills*—Ability to ask questions which elicit useful data or assumptions.
- *Conflict resolution skills.*
- *Oral and written communication skills.*

Financial and Policy Analysis Skills. Budget analysts should be able to think analytically. In other words, they should be able to break a complex problem into its component parts, look for patterns in data, and find the distinguishing characteristics between alternatives. Specifically, budget analysts should possess the following skill set:

1. Understand analytical concepts.
   a. Adjusting for inflation.
   b. Time value of money and discounting to present value.
   c. Unit cost.
   d. Sunk cost.
   e. Opportunity cost.
   f. Fixed and variable cost.
   g. Differential cost.
   h. Marginal cost.
   i. Basic statistics (average, median, standard deviation, correlation, scatter plots, etc.).
2. Proficiency with analysis tools and techniques.
   a. Basic techniques for comparing alternatives: decision tables, expected value tables, weighted score tables, decision trees.
   b. Advanced analytical techniques: break-even analysis, net present value analysis, return on investment analysis, cost-benefit analysis, fiscal impact analysis, cost-effectiveness analysis, sensitivity analysis.
   c. Expenditure and revenue analysis and forecasting.
   d. Budget variance analysis.
   e. Financial condition analysis (e.g., ICMA Financial Trend Monitoring System, 10 point test of financial condition).

f. Performance measurement—Developing performance measures and analyzing performance measurement data.

g. Performance auditing—Assess a program's efficiency and measure the extent to which it meets its goals and objectives.

h. Program evaluation—While performance measurement is systematic, regular, and government-wide, program evaluation is focused on a particular program, in-depth, and ad hoc.

i. Management analysis—Analyze work methods and organization of operating departments.

j Capital improvement programming—Assess capital needs, assess financial capacity including debt capacity, evaluate potential capital projects, plan projects and funding, develop capital budget, implement and monitor capital budget.

k. Cost accounting and cost analysis—(e.g., cost finding, indirect cost allocation, activity-based costing).

Familiarity with Innovations in Budgeting. Budget analysts should be familiar with best practices and innovations in state and local budgeting. Several of the most important innovations include:

1. NACSLB recommended practices
2. GFOA Budget Awards program
3. GFOA Recommended Practices
4. Long-term financial planning, multi-year budgeting, budgeting for structural balance
5. Strategic planning
6. Alternative budget formats (e.g., program, performance, and zero-base budgets).

MANAGING BUDGET OFFICE STAFF

Coordinating Complex and Unpredictable Budget Office Work

Budget office work can frequently be very complex, requiring a very high level of coordination and communication between employees. The management literature suggests the following four strategies to facilitate coordination in this type of environment: 1) reduce the amount of information that must be processed, 2) increase the capacity of leaders to handle more information and coordination, 3) increase the communication between subordinates, and 4) professionalize the workforce.

Strategy 1: Reduce Information Overload. Using the first strategy, the amount of information that must be processed can be reduced by grouping employees by their need to coordinate rather than by their profession. Grouping employees in the same unit simplifies communication and coordination (e.g., grouping budget analysts responsible for capital project planning). Another approach is to build more slack into the system (e.g., extending deadlines, providing excess resources, etc.), which can cover up deficiencies in the communication system.

Strategy 2: Increase Capacity of Leaders. The second strategy is to increase the capacity of leaders to handle more information and coordination. The capacity of leaders can be strengthened with staff advisors who gather and synthesize information. Improved decision making procedures and technology can also increase the capacity of leaders to manage highly complex organizations.

Strategy 3: Increase Communication Between Subordinates. In many organizations, decisions and information flow vertically—up and down the hierarchy. However, if the task is excessively complex, it may be necessary for communication to "take a short cut" and flow directly between employees of different departments. This third strategy of increasing the communication between subordinates can be accomplished using technologies such as e-mail, group software, and automated workflow features in ERP software. Another approach to increasing horizontal communication in an organization is to create special liaison positions, that is, employees who have the responsibility to facilitate coordination and communication between units. A third approach is to create task forces—which are temporary groups of employees from separate units. Another approach is to create more permanent groups of employees from separate units—project teams and standing committees. Finally, an elaborate method of facilitating coordination between employees is to use a matrix organizational structure. An organization with a matrix structure uses two or more organizational charts simultaneously. One organizational chart is the traditional chart that groups employees by department or function. A second organizational chart groups employees by process or by their need to coordinate. Employees in a matrix structure can belong to two or more units and report to two or more "bosses."

Strategy 4: Professionalize the Workforce. A fourth strategy is to professionalize the workforce. Professional training and standards reduces reliance on super-managers or a complex, matrix structure by making employees self-managing. Professional training can remove the need for direct supervision, while an employee's desire to meet external professional standards can take the place of monitoring by supervisors.

Coordinating Subunits in Large Budget Offices

The budget office in large governments is typically organized into subunits that specialize in a particular area of budgeting such as capital budgeting, revenue forecasting, and program monitoring. Although specialization enables a budget office to develop experts in particular areas, it also creates the need to coordinate these experts. The need to coordinate specialists is especially acute in the budget office because of the interdependence between the operating budget and activities such as revenue forecasting and capital budgeting that may be organized in separate units. Budget offices in large governments use five strategies to integrate related activities with the operating budget:

- Standard operating procedures that require communication and coordination;
- Integrated divisions;
- A large number of divisions which tends to centralize authority;
- Special units in the budget office that act as coordinating bodies; and,
- A corporate culture that fosters communication and coordination.

Special Coordinating Units. The U.S. Government Office of Management and Budget, Commonwealth of Virginia, and New York City use special units within their budget offices to coordinate related activities. The Federal OMB has twenty-five units that specialize in specific Federal agencies and ten units that coordinate cross-cutting activities within the organization. The units that have a broad, coordinating role are:

- General Counsel
- Legislative Affairs
- Communications
- Administration

- Economic Policy
- Legislative Reference
- Budget Review
- Office of Federal Financial Management
- Office of Federal Procurement Policy
- Office of Information and Regulatory Affairs

The Office of Budget Review is the central coordinating body for the Federal government's budget. The Office of Economic Policy makes decisions on economic and forecasting assumptions. The Office of Federal Financial Management makes government-wide financial policies. These offices supply the rest of OMB with policies and assumptions that OMB will use to develop the budget.

The New York City OMB has a similar structure as the Federal OMB but on a smaller scale. The New York OMB's central coordinating unit is the Office of Budget Review (which shares the same name as a similar unit at the Federal OMB). The Office of Budget Review includes subunits for budget coordination, personnel planning and control, capital financial planning, and budget information systems. The structures of New York City's OMB and the Federal OMB satisfy the need both to integrate budget functions and have specialists of government agencies.

The Commonwealth of Virginia's Department of Planning & Budget has a Budget Operations division to coordinate budget activities within the office. The other divisions within the department focus on program evaluation or government functions such as education and public safety.

Integrated Divisions. Several large governments coordinate operating and capital budgeting by integrating these activities in the same division. Instead of organizing the budget office into an operating budget division and capital budget division, the Federal OMB, Commonwealth of Virginia, and the Cities of New York, Los Angeles, and Phoenix structure their budget offices into units that specialize in specific government agencies and combine capital and operating analysis within these units. The Federal government and the Commonwealth of Virginia assign to each of its budget analysts operating *and* capital responsibilities.

Many Divisions. Research of budget and finance offices has found that a greater number of divisions tends to increase the centralization of authority in the head of the department and thus, increase the coordination between divisions. In other words, more divisions actually creates more unity. This tends to occur because a greater number of divisions increases the chances that a decision will affect two or more divisions and require the intervention of the department head.[7] For example, the GFOA found that the City of Chicago OMB—which has ten divisions—tends to have greater coordination between divisions than the budget office in a comparable city that had only five divisions. In the City of Chicago, the large number of divisions tends to give the deputy budget director a more important coordinating role and diminishes the importance of each division.

Standard Operating Procedures. Some budget offices use standard operating procedures that require communication and coordination among related budget activities. For example, in the State of Maryland, the Department of Planning and Budget requires that capital budget items have an operating impact statement.

Corporate Culture. In many governments, the effective integration of activities is due primarily to a corporate culture that fosters communication and coordination. A budget director in the State of Maryland noted that integration and cooperation is part of the corporate culture within the budget office. The City of Chicago uses a team building exercise to foster a culture of cooperation and coordination. As part of office tradition, rookie budget analysts from all divisions create and perform a skit during the office's Christmas party.

Turnover and Personnel Retention

A high rate of turnover among budget analysts is a concern in many budget offices. Turnover can be caused by the "pull" of other job opportunities[8] and by the "push" of a negative situation in the budget office (e.g., a poorly designed job, negative environment, insufficient compensation for tasks, or a lack of non-material incentives). Three key factors that effect rates of turnover include:

1. Economic and labor market conditions—the state of the economy and the demand and supply of budget analysts
2. Circumstances in the budget office and government organization—e.g., morale, job design, and promotional opportunities.

3. Individual factors—career or lifestyle changes such as retirement, moving to another city, and changing careers.

Of these three factors, the most important factor behind high turnover rates for career professionals tends to be economic and labor market conditions.

Although there are significant factors that cause turnover, there are also substantial financial and nonfinancial incentives that managers can use to retain (and recruit) good employees. Five well-tested[9] strategies for retaining and recruiting employees include:

1. Material incentives (e.g., competitive salaries, pension, health care benefits).
2. Nonmaterial incentives (e.g., prestige, recognition, power).
3. Working conditions (e.g., bigger office, better equipment, flexibility to work at home, well structured workload, high quality budget manual and formalized procedures, direction and clear responsibilities).
4. Sense of an important, common purpose and the congeniality of the social environment (e.g., the importance of the budget process to the welfare of the community, team building, office friendships).
5. Inclusion in organizational decision making (e.g., analysts participate in development of budget proposal, improvement of budget process).

Of these five classes of incentives, the two that are usually most important to motivating budget analysts tend to be the sense of purpose and importance in participating in a community's budget process and the nonmaterial incentive of having influence over government programs and large departmental budgets.

Professional Development and Training

As discussed earlier, budget offices may experience more turnover than other government departments. An effective way to manage employees in an environment of high turnover with a high percentage of new employees is through professional development and training. Professional development and training is also a means to prevent high rates of turnover in the future.[10] For example, a high quality training and development program can decrease employee frustration and increase job satisfaction.

Training refers to a course or seminar taught by an instructor. Development refers to the process in which an employee learns on the job. Mentoring refers to an arrangement where an advisor provides a newer employee working for the same organization with the benefit of their experience.

Development, training, and mentoring work together. Employees tend to learn the most on their own through development. However, training and mentoring are necessary because they maximize the amount of learning that people can receive through development. Basically, training and mentoring prepare a person's mind to learn efficiently on their own. Without adequate training and mentoring, some employees may learn little through development. From the other direction, without adequate development and an opportunity to immediately use the information that is learned, training may have little result.

The following are several training and development strategies:

1. Internal training—Internal training is training conducted by the organization itself on the processes, procedures, forms, and responsibilities *specific to the government*. An example of this form of training is an orientation program for new analysts. For training to be effective, it should be accompanied with written instructions such as an orientation manual and/or budget procedures manual.

2. External training—External training is conducted by individuals from outside the organization. It tends to be general in scope. External training may teach topics such as: general analytical skills, oral and written communication skills, government accounting, and best practices. This type of training is necessary for analysts to enhance their skill sets and possess the analytical tools for conducting policy and program analysis. (See Appendix B for a list of GFOA training resources for budget analysts.)

3. Training budget—A designated budget for training is an important way to make training a priority. A tuition reimbursement policy is another means of providing financial support to training.

4. Formal mentoring system—Although some employees may seek a mentor on their own, a formal system should be used to ensure that all new employees benefit from a mentor.
5. Professional conferences—Conferences can be an efficient way to survey the latest developments in the field of budgeting.
6. Publications—Handbooks and guidebooks from outside organizations can be an effective and very inexpensive way for budget analysts to obtain an overview of budget processes, learn how to use analysis tools, and learn other important skills. (See Appendix B for a list of GFOA publications in public budgeting.)

BUDGET OFFICE SIZES IN STATE GOVERNMENTS AND MAJOR LOCAL GOVERNMENTS

This section documents the typical size of budget offices in state governments and major local governments. The results of two recent studies found that state governments have an average of about *two* budget office staff for each $1 billion in total expenditures, while major local governments have about *ten* budget office staff per $1 billion. Thus, state governments tend to have smaller budget offices than major local governments of the same size. Apparently, state governments tend to experience significant economies of scale in the staffing of their budget offices as the total state budget increases from $2 to $10 billion.

Comparisons of budget office sizes should be treated with caution. The staff and expenditures of a budget office are primarily a function of the size of the government, the scope of responsibilities of the budget office, and the extent to which the budgeting function is centralized. Because governments differ in size, and budget offices differ in scope and centralization, it is difficult to compare their staffing and expenditures. However, an attempt is made here to compare budget offices with similar sizes and responsibilities using expenditure and staffing data from each government.

Major City and County Governments. The following benchmarks were used to measure the size of budget offices in major local governments:

- Budget office expenditures as a percentage of total government expenditures;

Exhibit 4-1 ■ Budget Office Sizes in Major Local Governments[11]

Benchmark	Average	Range
Budget office expenditures as a percentage of total government expenditures	0.10%	0.07% to 0.19%
Budget office staff as a percentage of total government employment	0.19%	0.09% to 0.47%
Budget office staff per $1 billion of total government expenditures	10.0	4.5 to 17.8

- Budget office staff as a percentage of total government employment; and,
- Budget office staff per $1 billion of total government expenditures.

To calculate ratios that can be compared across governments of different sizes, these benchmarks divide budget office expenditures or staff by the government's total expenditures or employment. Although the budget offices differ in responsibilities, an attempt was made to isolate the expenditures and staff for a comparable set of responsibilities in each budget office. For example, the estimates of budget office staff and expenditures exclude budget office units with unusual responsibilities not performed by all of the governments in the sample such as intergovernmental relations, employee relations, human resources, and management information systems.

The three benchmarks in Exhibit 4-1 show that budget offices differ widely in their staffing and departmental expenditures. For example, the budget office staff per $1 billion in total government expenditures ranges from 4.5 staff to 17.8 staff per $1 billion. The average number of staff is 10.0 staff per $1 billion in total government expenditures. This is equivalent to assigning each staff member about $100 million in departmental expenditures.[12] It should be restated that these results should be treated with caution as it is very difficult to make comparisons between governments.

State Governments. The following benchmarks were used to measure the size of budget offices in state governments:

- Budget function positions per $1 billion of total state expenditures;
- Budget analysts per $1 billion of total state expenditures;
- Budget function positions as a percentage of total state employment (FTEs); and,

Exhibit 4-2 ■ Budget Office Sizes in State Governments[13]

Benchmark	Average	Range
Budget function positions per $1 billion of total state expenditures	2.4	0.5 to 9.2
Budget analysts per $1 billion of total state expenditures	1.6	0.4 to 5.5
Budget function positions as a percentage of total state employment (FTEs)	0.048%	0.010% to 0.145%
Budget analysts as a percentage of total state employment (FTEs)	0.031%	0.007% to 0.109%

- Budget analysts as a percentage of total state employment (FTEs).

To enable comparisons between states of different sizes, these benchmarks divide budget office staff by the state government's total expenditures or employment. "Budget function positions" includes analysts, support personnel, and computer staff.

Exhibit 4-2 shows that state governments tend to have smaller budget offices than major cities. While major cities tend to have an average of 10.0 budget staff per $1 billion in total government expenditures, state budget offices have an average of 2.4 budget staff per $1 billion. Even the smallest states—which are similar in size to many large cities—have an average of about 4.1 budget staff per $1 billion. Although future study is needed, it may be that state governments have relatively small budget offices because they generally have a much more decentralized budget process than major cities of comparable size.

Exhibit 4-3 shows that state budget offices experience significant economies of scale as the total state government expenditures increases from $2 to $10 billion. For example, states with a total expenditure of $2 to $5 billion have an average of 4.10 budget function positions per $1 billion. This number drops to 1.89 budget function positions per $1 billion for states with a total expenditure of $10 to $15 billion.

SUMMARY

This chapter discussed key issues related to the staffing of the budget office. Public budgeting has undergone several dramatic changes in the past forty years. These changes include: a revolution in information technology, more complex government services, a political climate re-

Exhibit 4-3 ▪ Economies of Scale in State Budget Offices[14]

Total State Government Expenditures	Average Budget Function Positions per $1 Billion	Average Budget Analysts per $1 Billion	Average Budget Function Positions as % of Total FTEs	Average Budget Analysts as % of Total FTEs
$2 to $5 Billion	4.10	2.55	0.073%	0.047%
$5 to $10 Billion	2.39	1.64	0.042%	0.028%
$10 to $15 Billion	1.89	1.23	0.037%	0.024%
$15 to $20 Billion	1.91	1.22	0.043%	0.028%
$20 to $25 Billion	1.55	1.17	0.031%	0.023%
$25 Billion +	1.58	0.98	0.046%	0.028%

sistant to new taxes, innovations in budgeting techniques, and the proliferation of education and training opportunities for budget analysts. An effective budget office should have budget analysts with skills, knowledge, and abilities that match today's environment. Budget analysts should:

- Understand their government's finances and operations;
- Have effective "people skills" with political savvy and excellent communication skills;
- Be able to think analytically, understand analytical concepts, and be proficient with analysis tools and techniques; and,
- Be familiar with innovations and best practices in state and local budgeting.

This chapter also discussed management strategies for coordinating budget office work, retaining good employees, and training employees. The chapter concluded by discussing the typical number of budget office staff in state governments and major local governments.

Endnotes

1. Anthony Rainey, "The Technology Fast Track: Anticipating and Coping with Change," GFOA Conference: The Finance Officer and The Communities of Tomorrow, June 2, 1997.
2. *Trends in State and Local Government Spending*, Program Evaluation Division, Office of the Legislative Auditor, State of Minnesota, Report Number: 96-03 (February 13, 1996), 14.
3. A survey of 510 GFOA members found that 51 percent of the respondents use a line-item format, 35 percent use a hybrid format, 10 percent use a program budget format, 3 percent use a

performance based budget format, and 2 percent use a zero-base budget format. Source: Daniel E. O'Toole, James Marshall, and Timothy Grewe, "Current Local Government Budgeting Practices," *Government Finance Review* 12 (December 1996), 27.

4. Some of the material in this section is based on GFOA national seminar presentations given by Maria Kwiatkowski and Roland Calia.

5. Of course, it should be noted that many of these skills, knowledge, and abilities are learned on the job. Thus interpersonal and analytical skills naturally grow over time through experience, on-the-job training, and formal, off-site training.

6. Examples of political factors that shape the budget include: leaders' preferences, reelection pressures on leadership, interest group pressure, citizen preferences, interests of budget program clientele and constituencies, operating department interests, labor union interests, and the media.

7. This is based on a GFOA study of 254 local government finance organizations. Source: Marshall W. Meyer, "Centralization and Decentralization of Authority in Departments of Finance," *Municipal Finance* (August 1967): 40-46.

8. The broad organizational involvement and excellent skill set of experienced budget professionals tends to make them highly sought after by other departments within their government and by other organizations.

9. This list is based on Chester Barnard's classic book, *The Functions of the Executive* (Cambridge: Harvard University Press, 1968, originally published in 1938).

10. It is also possible, however, that professional development and training can *increase* turnover by making employees more attractive to other employers. This may occur when other employers can offer better financial and nonfinancial incentives.

11. Sample: Budget offices in nine major U.S. cities. Source: GFOA Research and Consulting Center survey, fall 2000. This analysis only applies to major governments with a total expenditure greater than one billion dollars.

12. It should be noted that this analysis includes all *funded* positions, not just filled positions, and includes support personnel and directors in addition to budget analysts.

13. *Budget Processes in the States* (National Association of State Budget Officers, October 1999), 12-13. Total state employment and expenditure data from the U.S. Census of Governments, March 1998. The ratios were calculated by the author.

14. *Budget Processes in the States*, 12-13. Total state employment and expenditure data from the U.S. Census of Governments, March 1998. The ratios were calculated by the author.

CHAPTER 5

Implementing NACSLB Practices on Coordinating the Budget Process

This chapter will show how to implement four of the recommended practices of the National Advisory Council on State and Local Budgeting (NACSLB). The NACSLB is a cooperative effort of eight state and local government associations to improve governmental budgeting. To achieve this goal, the NACSLB developed a comprehensive set of 59 recommended practices. These budgeting practices cover all steps of the budgeting process including the analysis and goal setting that occurs before the written budget document is produced, the items that should be included in the budget document, and the monitoring and evaluation that occurs after the document is adopted.

The focus of this book—the organization and design of the budget function—falls within element eight of the NACSLB framework of recommended practices. Element eight, "Develop a Process for Preparing and Adopting a Budget," concentrates on the administrative structure and coordination tools (i.e., budget calendars and budget instruction manuals) that governments should use to coordinate the budget process. In its broadest sense, the budget function includes not only the direct participants in the budget process, but also stakeholders such as citizens and the news media. For this reason, this chapter also covers methods of obtaining stakeholder input into the budget process. Each section in this chapter shows how to implement one of the following four budget practices:

- Practice 8.1—Develop a Budget Calendar;
- Practice 8.2—Develop Budget Guidelines and Instructions;
- Practice 8.3—Develop Mechanisms for Coordinating Budget Preparation and Review;
- Practice 8.5—Identify Opportunities for Stakeholder Input.

BUDGET PRACTICE 8.1—DEVELOP A BUDGET CALENDAR

This budget practice recommends that governments publish a comprehensive budget calendar that specifies when budget tasks are to be completed and that identifies timelines for those tasks. A budget calendar serves the following purposes:

- Provides a "big picture" view of the budget process which can help to ensure that all aspects of the budget process have been considered and that adequate time has been provided to meet deadlines;
- Highlights important statutory deadlines;
- Coordinates the preparation of the budget and keeps participants on track;
- Informs stakeholders when key budget tasks, events, and decisions will occur so they have an opportunity to plan and to participate in the process.

What Should Be Included in a Budget Calendar. A budget calendar should list the dates of key activities and deadlines. It should also identify who is responsible for each activity. The dates for the following activities[1] should be included in a budget calendar:

- Distribution of budget worksheets, instructions, and guidelines to departments;
- Preparation of expenditure estimates;
- Preparation of revenue estimates;
- Submission of departmental budget requests to the budget officer;

- Compilation of budget requests into budget document and completion of summary schedules;
- Chief executive review of budget requests;
- Budget presentation to legislative body;
- Release of drafts of new ordinances;
- Budget hearings and other opportunities in which stakeholders can participate;
- Adoption of budget; and,
- Beginning of new fiscal year.

Typically, a government will need to produce multiple versions of its budget calendar to meet the needs of different users such as citizens, elected officials, and operating departments.

The remainder of this section includes two examples of this practice:

- Exhibit 5-1—A Budget Calendar that Clearly Identifies Participants.

  In this budget calendar, Volusia County, Florida clearly identifies the participants responsible for each item in the budget process.

- Exhibit 5-2—A Budget Checklist.

  This supplement to Glendale's budget calendar clearly identifies the specific responsibilities of each participant in the budget process.

Exhibit 5-1 ■ A Budget Calendar that Clearly Identifies Participants[2]

Date	Responsible	Event
January 10 — February 9	Budget	FY 1999-2000 Fourth Quarter Analysis
February 5 – February 28	Budget	FY 2000-01 Second Quarter Analysis
March 8	County Council	FY 2000-01 Quarterly Analysis, Budget Calendar
March 12	Budget	Access Budget Training for all Service Groups; Distribution of Budget Preparation Packages
April 5	County Council	Five Year Forecast, FY 2001-02 Budget Issues
March 12 – April 20	Service Groups/Activities	Prepare Budget Requests
April 20 – May 18	Budget	Prepare Preliminary Recommended Budget and Decision Packages for County Manager/Service Center Directors Proposed Budget Meeting
May 21 – May 25	County Manager/ Service Center Directors	Budget Meeting on Final Budget Decisions
June	Property Appraiser	Preliminary Tax Roll Data
June 4 – July 3	Budget	Prepare Recommended Budget
June 29	Property Appraiser	Certifies Tax Roll
July 12	County Manager	Recommended Budget distributed to County Council
July 12 – September 5	County Council	Reviews Recommended Budget - Workshops
July 30 – August 17	Budget	Third Quarter analysis
August 2	County Council	Adoption of TRIM Rates
August 4	Budget	Statutory deadline to notify Property Appraiser of Proposed TRIM Rates and the Date, Time, and Place of the First Public Hearing to Adopt the Budget
August 24	Property Appraiser	Last Day to Mail TRIM Notices
September 6	County Council	First Public Hearing - Adopt Tentative Budget and Millage Rates, Set Final Public Hearing Date, Time, and Place
September 16	Budget	Advertise Final Budget and Millage Hearing
September 20	County Council	Final Public Hearing to Adopt the FY 2001-02 Millage Rates and Budget
September 21	Budget	Certified Copy of Adopted Millage Resolution to Property Appraiser and Chief Financial Officer
Typically after Value Adjustment Board	Property Appraiser	Issue Certification of Final Taxable Value
Not later than 3 days after receipt of Final Taxable Value	Budget	Complete Certification of Final Taxable Value and Return to Property Appraiser
October 19	Budget	Within 30 Days of Adopting Final Budget Certify to the Department of Revenue compliance with TRIM (F.S. Chapter 200)

Exhibit 5-2 ■ A Budget Checklist[3]

Division Managers

_____ Attend budget orientation on 1/2/2001

_____ Attend budget preparation workshop by 1/5/2001

_____ Prepare budget forms and narratives. Submit them to your Deputy/Assistant City Manager and the Budget Office by 2/2/2001. The required materials are:

    _____ Base Budget Input Form to be entered into system

    _____ Carryover Savings Allocation Form to be entered into system

    _____ Supplemental Request Form (if applicable) to be entered into system

    _____ Program Narratives

    _____ Budget Training Survey—located in Budget Input System

Department Heads

_____ Attend Budget Orientation on 1/2/2001

_____ Establish a process with your division managers for review of the departmental budget during the week of 1/26/2001

_____ Adjust divisions' base budget and carryover budgets as necessary to address imbalances

_____ Submit edited forms to your Deputy/Assistant City Manager by 2/2/2001

_____ Submit budget narratives, performance indicators and graphical information to your Deputy/Assistant City Manager and the Budget Office by 2/2/2001. (Each department is **REQUIRED** to have a graph included in their narrative. Please provide the data and the Budget staff will do the graphing)

_____ Review supplementals with your Deputy/Assistant City Manager Deputy/Assistant City Manager

_____ Set-up a process with department heads and division managers for review of the group's budget following the week of 2/2/2001. Inform the Budget Office of the meeting date.

_____ Adjust base budgets and carryover budgets as necessary to address imbalances

    _____ Provide FINAL list of supplementals to the Budget Office by 2/16/2001

BUDGET PRACTICE 8.2—DEVELOP BUDGET GUIDELINES AND INSTRUCTIONS

This budget practice recommends that governments prepare budget guidelines and detailed budget preparation instructions for each budget cycle. Budget guidelines are a general set of policies regarding budget increases and service levels for the upcoming budget. Unlike the government's financial policies, budget guidelines are specific to the financial and operating conditions in a particular budget year. Governments use the general policies in its budget guidelines to prepare a budget instruction manual, which provides departments with more specific instructions and forms to prepare budget requests.

Budget guidelines and instructions serve several purposes. They ensure that the budget is consistent with the policies and direction of the chief executive and legislative body. By communicating the expectations of the leadership, they minimize misunderstanding and extra work by participants in the budget process. Finally, they facilitate the evaluation of department budget requests by forcing departments to submit their requests in a standard format, following government-wide assumptions regarding inflation rates, tax rates, etc.

How to Prepare Budget Guidelines.[4] Preparing budget guidelines involves the following steps:

1. Assess likely financial constraints in the budget year. Use data from the current year and estimates of the upcoming year to determine the financial constraints. Key factors to consider include:
   a. Revenues
   b. Expenditures
   c. Trends in inflation and local economic conditions
   d. Prospects for new taxes and fees
   e. Major cost items that will fall due in the budget year.

2. Assess service needs. Discuss desired service levels in the budget year with department heads.

3. Develop budget policies. Based on the assessments of financial constraints and service needs, the chief executive and legislative body should develop budget policies to guide the development of the budget. These policies may include:

    a. Guidelines for budget increases due to inflation;

    b. A range for cost-of-living adjustments to salaries of municipal employees;

    c. An indication of what service areas should be strengthened, de-emphasized, or reduced, and,

    d. A statement of tax and fee policies to be followed.

4. Legislative body formally endorses policies.

5. Disseminate policies to all appropriate administrative officials.

How to Prepare a Budget Instruction Manual. The budget instruction manual is a set of detailed instructions given to each department for preparing the budget. This manual should be given to department officials a sufficient period in advance of when budgets are due. A budget instruction manual should include the following items:[5]

1. A statement from the chief executive or budget officer summarizing the anticipated fiscal position of the government and an outline of overall fiscal polices to be pursued. The budget officer should encourage department heads to examine the merit of existing programs and to justify requests for new or expanded programs fully.

2. A description of the budget process.

3. A budget calendar indicating dates of all pertinent activities relating to the completion of the budget.

4. Assumptions that all departments should use in their analyses—The rate of inflation to be used in estimating costs, discount rate for net present value analyses, current prices of office equipment and supplies, internal service charges, and other factors that would apply to all departments across the board.

5. Forms—Copies of all forms to be completed along with detailed instructions and examples of how to complete them. These forms also can be used as formats for presentation of budget recommendations to the legislative body. Computer spreadsheets can be used to prepare this information in electronic form. This process makes it easier to prepare the budget document later and it may be possible to transfer departmental data electronically. The types of forms needed include:

- Detailed worksheets for personal services, operating expenditures, and capital requests;
- A worksheet detailing proposed expenditures for each activity and sources of funds to support the activity (e.g., general funds, federal funds, and special revenues);
- Forms to summarize various expenditure categories into departmental and program totals; and,
- A statement of the role the budget officer intends to play in budget development, including: assisting departments in preparing requests, responding to questions about policy or procedure, and clarifying any ambiguities in the instructions.

6. Expenditure and revenue codes.
7. Other information—A description of the budget transfer process, glossary, explanation of financial reports, employee counts and classifications, and telephone numbers.

The remainder of this section includes two examples of this practice:

- Exhibit 5-3—A Budget Preparation Manual
  This example shows the contents of Jackson County's budget preparation manual, which includes a 14 step process for budget preparation.
- Exhibit 5-4—Instructions for Completing Budget Forms
  This excerpt from the Hillsborough County, Florida budget manual is a good example of including instructions on how to complete budget forms. The County's budget manual also includes instructions for three other budget forms, and examples of completed forms.

Exhibit 5-3 ■ A Budget Preparation Manual[6]

Table of Contents

Exhibit 5-4 ■ Instructions for Completing Budget Forms

COMPLETING THE FY 02 AND FY 03 DECISION UNIT DESCRIPTION AND COST FORM (BF002)

Information on how to complete form BF002 is presented in eight sections and corresponds to the large numbered section on a copy of the form.

Section 1: For organizations that report to the County Administrator, note the Office your department is associated with (i.e., Human Services, Community Services or Management Services). For all organizations identify the title of the organization in the blank space to the right of *Department*.

Section 2: In the space to the right of the term *Fund* provide the full fund notation. The full notation for a fund links both the fund type and fund, such as the Enterprise Funds, Utility System Revenue Bonds Fund (40-040). In the space provided to the right of the term **Subfund**, complete the reference with the three-digit subfund number, such as 001 for the Utility System Operation and Maintenance Account. Other examples follow:

Examples:

Fund: 01-001   Countywide General Fund
Subfund: 001   Operating Fund

Fund: 10-002   Countywide Special
              Purpose Revenue Fund
Subfund: 727   Court Technology Trust
              Fund

Fund: 01-003   Unincorporated Area
              General Fund
Subfund: 001   Operating Fund

In the space provided to the right of the term **Index Code**, complete the reference with the eight-digit index code number or numbers as appropriate. An example would be FRE03000 for Fire Suppression Operations.

Section 3: Identify the service level of the decision unit using one of the following categories: Minimum Service Level (MSL), Continuation, New Mandate or Desired Service.

Section 4: Identify the priority position of all decision units (1 or 5 or 12, etc.). Decision Units are to be prioritized both within a specific funding source as well as overall by department. Priorities at the department level should be unique. A department will only have one priority #3 and one priority #5, etc. This includes all Minimum Service Level Decision Units.

Section 5: If a particular decision unit pertains to the funding of the operation, maintenance, or start-up cost of a new facility or improvement then identify the corresponding CIP number(s) in this area. If this decision unit is not associated with a Capital Improvement Project then indicate such as N/A.

Section 6: In response to a recommendation by the Blue Ribbon Committee on County Finances, the BOCC requested that a matrix be developed which would classify the services provided by Hillsborough County as mandatory, essential, or discretionary. The original list was published in conjunction with the FY 00 and FY 01 biennial budget and is republished in this document for reference. In the space provided, identify the category code of M1, M2, E, or D to reflect whether the service is mandated, essential or discretionary as defined on pages 36 - 44. If you reflect a service that is not listed on the Service Matrix, please do your best with regard to identifying the appropriate service category.

Section 7: Give each decision unit some short distinct title. This short description should be used on the summary form to identify the decision unit when the summary ranking is compiled.

Section 8: Many times it is unclear as to which service or function a particular Decision Unit belongs. In the area of the form adjacent to **Service**, provide a general description of the related service being provided (i.e. Fire Suppression, Water Distribution, Library Circulation).

Exhibit 5-4 ■ Instructions for Completing Budget Forms (Continued)

FY 02 and FY 03 DECISION UNIT
DESCRIPTION & COST

Office	
Department	(1)

Fund	
Subfund	(2)
Index Code	

SERVICE LEVEL
_____ (3)

CATEGORY: (6)
(M1, M2, E, D)

PRIORITY	
Funding Source Priority #:	(4)
Department Priority #:	

CIP #: (5)

BUDGETARY DECISION UNIT: (7) _____

SERVICE: _____ (8) _____

RESOURCES:

	Total Costs			Total Positions (listed by job class)		
	FY 02	FY 02		Class #	Description	FY 02 FY 03
Personal Services						
Operating Expenses	(9)			(10)		
Capital Outlay						
TOTAL				TOTAL	0.0 0.0	

IMPACT ON FY02:

(11)

IMPACT ON FY02 (if different from FY 02):

(12)

REVENUE IMPACT:

Revenue Description	FY02	FY03	Narrative:
		(13)	

BUDGET PRACTICE 8.3—DEVELOP MECHANISMS FOR COORDINATING BUDGET PREPARATION AND REVIEW

This budget practice focuses on how the budget process is coordinated. It recommends that governments develop a way to coordinate the budget process. A single point of coordination is often appropriate in local governments. The coordinator should have immediate access to decision makers. Coordination is necessary to prevent confusion and misinformation, ensure that the budget process moves forward as planned, and ensure that appropriate stakeholders are involved.

The Scope and Tasks of Budget Process Coordination.[7] Depending on the government, the responsibilities given to the budget coordinator may vary in scope. At a minimum, the coordinator should be given responsibility for the basic coordination of the budget process—such as keeping the process on schedule, designing standard forms, and verifying the accuracy and completeness of budget requests. The coordinator might also be given a larger, policy guidance role—such as evaluating department requests, making recommendations, and balancing revenues and expenditures. In addition to these responsibilities, the coordinator may also be given responsibility for monitoring the implementation of the budget.

Basic Coordination. Basic coordination of the budget process includes coordinating the activities and deadlines in the budget process and standardizing forms and worksheets to facilitate the integration of budget material. Specifically, the responsibility for basic coordination includes:

1. Developing the budget calendar or schedule.
2. Identifying responsibilities in the budget process.
3. Designing budget worksheets and forms.
4. Assisting departments to formalize performance measures (if applicable).
5. Developing budget worksheet instructions for department heads.
6. Reviewing finished worksheets for accuracy and completeness.
7. Preparing or assembling revenue estimates.

8. Presenting budgetary materials to the chief executive for review.

9. Assisting the chief executive to prepare a recommended budget for elected officials.

10. Coordinating activities, scheduling meetings, and keeping the process on schedule.

11. Ensuring that the parts of the budget process are properly integrated.

12. Identifying issues and problems.

Policy Guidance. In addition to basic coordination, the budget coordinator may also perform significant analytical and policy guidance functions such as evaluating department requests, balancing revenues and expenditures, and making recommendations to the chief executive. In this larger role, the budget coordinator helps to shape the *substance* of the budget, not just the *process* of the budget. Specific policy guidance responsibilities include:

1. Issuing guidelines to departmental officials regarding acceptable levels of service increases or decreases and expected cost limitations.

2. Evaluating departmental requests and adjusting them to policy guidelines.

3. Developing the budget objectives of the locality including any constraints which may be imposed.

4. Ensuring consistency of requests within and among departments.

5. Balancing expenditure request with available revenues.

6. Making recommendations for budget action to the legislative body.

Supervision of Budget Implementation. After a budget has been adopted, the budget coordinator may also be given the responsibility to supervise the implementation of the budget. In this role, the budget coordinator monitors departmental spending, reviews budget transfer requests, and generates regular, mid-year budget reports. Specific budget implementation responsibilities include:

1. Ensuring that departments do not exceed budget limits by conducting periodic projections of expenditures and comparing them to available resources.

2. Reviewing all requests to transfer from one budget item to another.

3. Maintaining and updating the manual of budget procedures.

4. Preparing reports on budgetary performance for the legislative body, chief executive, and departments.

5. Closely monitoring departmental performance to determine potential adverse trends.

Single Point of Coordination. For most local governments, a single point of coordination is often appropriate. The coordinator may be an administrator with part time budgeting responsibilities or a full time budget director. There are a number of advantages of a single budget coordinator with a broad set of responsibilities including responsibility for basic coordination, policy guidance, and budget implementation. Some of these advantages are:

1. Priorities for services can best be determined from a central vantage point;

2. Budget preparation is facilitated through standardization of procedures and forms;

3. Effective control of local government resources can be achieved more easily since the inflow and outflow of these resources is handled through one official;

4. Fiscal problems can be detected sooner because an official with budgetary and financial experience reviews departments' service levels in a timely manner; and,

5. Budget implementation is facilitated by the use of standard forms for all budget actions—such as submitting requests for transfer of funds, new positions, or changes in existing positions.[8]

Current Practice. Most local governments with a budget office make it a single point of coordination for basic coordination, policy guidance, and budget implementation. A survey of 510 local government budget offices[9] found that 88 percent to 99 percent have responsibility for the following activities:

1. Packaging the proposed budget;

2. Analyzing department requests;

3. Formulating revenue estimates;

4. Monitoring department expenditures; and,

5. Making allocation recommendations.

A survey of large city and county governments in the U.S.[10] found that nearly all (90% – 100%) of the budget offices in the sample have the full responsibility for the following activities:

1. Preparing forecasts of revenues and expenditures;

2. Monitoring capital budget;

3. Preparing budget guidelines and instructions;

4. Preparing proposed budget;

5. Monitoring departmental budget execution; and,

6. Recommending mid-year budget adjustments.

Immediate Access to Decision Makers. The budget coordinator should have immediate access to decision makers. One common organizational method of giving the budget coordinator access to decision makers is to separate the budget office from the rest of the finance organization and give the budget director a direct reporting relationship with the chief executive. In this arrangement the budget office may be located in the chief executive's office or may be a freestanding agency.

There are several advantages to giving the budget director a direct reporting relationship with the chief executive. First, it allows the chief executive direct control over a government's budget because the budget director reports to him or her rather than to a CFO. Thus, the budget office is positioned to carry out the chief executive's priorities and vision. Second, the budget office may have a more active role in policy development because of its proximity to the city's chief policy-maker. Third, the budget office is better suited to integrate decision making, priority setting, and the budget process. Finally, the budgeting function may be given a higher priority by the chief executive than if it were a subfunction under a CFO. About thirty percent of local governments place the budget office in the chief executive's office or as a separate department. However, as a jurisdiction's size increases, its budget office is more likely to be a separate department reporting directly to the chief executive.[11]

The remainder of this section includes three examples of this practice:

- Exhibit 5-5—Assignment of Budget Roles in the City of Scottsdale, Arizona

- Exhibit 5-6—Assignment of Budget Roles in Waukesha County, Wisconsin
- Exhibit 5-7—Assignment of Budget Roles in the City of San Luis Obispo, California

Exhibit 5-5 ■ Assignment of Budget Roles in the City of Scottsdale, Arizona[12]

Budget Roles and Responsibilities

Every employee plays a role in budgeting - whether in its formulation, preparation, implementation, administration, or evaluation. Ultimately, of course, each general manager, through the City Manager, is accountable to the City Council for the performance of departmental personnel in meeting specific objectives within allocated resource limits.

Actual budget responsibility can be identified more specifically:

- The program *Center Manager* is responsible for preparing an estimate of remaining cost requirements for the current fiscal year, projecting the base budget requirements for the next fiscal year, and developing other requests that change or revise the program so that it will be more effective, efficient, productive, and economical.

- The *Budget Liaisons* serve as the vital communication link between the departments and the budget staff. Liaisons are responsible for coordinating information, checking to see if forms are completed properly, making sure that all necessary documentation is submitted, monitoring the internal review process to meet timelines, and serving as troubleshooters for problems throughout the budget process.

- The *Capital Improvement Plan Coordination Team* is comprised of staff from various City departments. The team is responsible for reviewing all capital projects for timing and cost considerations, compiling lifecycle costs, and preparing a preliminary capital improvement plan recommendation for review and revision by the General Managers, City Manager, City Council and various boards and commissions staffed by citizens.

- The *Division Directors, General Manager, and Charter Officers* are responsible for reviewing historical performance, anticipating future problems and opportunities, considering alternative solutions, and modifying and assembling their departmental data into a cohesive budget information package. General Managers critically evaluate all requests, prioritize, and submit a balanced budget plan including only those requests which support Council policies, City Manager workplan, administrative direction, and departmental mission.

- The *Budget Manager* and staff within the Accounting and Budget division are responsible for preparing short- and long-range revenue and expenditure forecasts and calculating departmental budget targets. Assistance is provided to departmental general managers or staff with preparation requirements and with presentation formats. Budget staff also coordinates the collating, analyzing, and summarizing departmental requests and preparing budget review materials for the Executive Team, Mayor, and City Council.

- The *Budget Director, City Treasurer, and Assistant City Managers'* key role is translating Mayor and City Council goals and objectives for the City into recommended funding decisions. They are responsible for reviewing the departmental operating and CIP requests and submitting their recommendations for review by the Executive Team, Mayor and Council.

- The *City Manager* is responsible for reviewing the total financial program and formulating a City-wide tentative budget and submitting it to the Mayor and City Council.

- The *Mayor and City Council* are responsible for the review of the City Manager's tentative budget and approval of the final budget.

Exhibit 5-6 ■ Assignment of Budget Roles in Waukesha County, Wisconsin[13]

The preparation of the annual operating budget represents a cooperative effort. The responsibilities of the various departments are detailed below.

It is the responsibility of the <u>County Executive</u> to:

A. Present an Executive Budget to the County Board of Supervisors.

B. Deliver a budget message to the County Board.

C. May veto items added by County Board amendment.

It is the responsibility of the <u>County Board of Supervisors</u> to:

A. Hold County Board and Committee reviews on the budget.

B. Hold a Public Hearing on the budget.

C. Adopt the budget, addressing amendments advanced for County Board actions.

D. Hold a budget meeting to address County Executive's vetoes if necessary.

E. Hold annual post-budget feedback session to address improvements to process and information provided.

It is the responsibility of the <u>DOA – Budget Division</u> to:

A. Develop the budget reporting format on the County's computer system. Plan for and determine informational needs for policy makers from annual post-budget feedback session to assist in the annual operating budget review process.

B. Issue Executive-established budget targets and forms to be used by County departments for development and presentation of their respective operating budget for the ensuing year.

C. Review and analyze budget requests for accuracy and for compliance with established instructions. Particular attention is paid to:

   1. Reviewing the department's strategic objectives, accomplishments, program highlights and position summary.

   2. Examining the expenditure and revenue assumptions upon which the department has built its budget request.

   3. Determining if expenditures are budgeted at realistic levels and revenues are budgeted at somewhat conservative and achievable levels.

   4. Determining cost effectiveness of programs or services.

   5. Determining whether or not a department has achieved its established budget target.

D. Meet with department administrators and/or their fiscal staff to discuss key budget issues.

E. Update and prepare the budget forms with County Board action for presentation in the annual County Board Adopted Budget document.

F. Verify that all line item detail is consistent and ties to the final adopted budget appropriations.

G. Coordinate, in conjunction with the DOA - Accounting and Information Systems divisions the "roll over" of budget line item detail into the financial system general ledger to prepare for the ensuing fiscal year.

Exhibit 5-6 ■ Assignment of Budget Roles in Waukesha County, Wisconsin (Continued)

It is the responsibility of the <u>department administrators and their staff</u> to:

A. Review Separate **Budget Instructions** and Procedures Manual and attend appropriate budget training.

B. Develop budget request and complete all required forms according to the specific instructions and time line (See **Budget Instructions**).

C. Prepare the budget in the prescribed **Performance Based/Program Cost Budget** format (See **Budget Instructions**). The Performance Based/Program Cost budget format focuses on the identification of expenditures and revenues for major services and programs leading to a better understanding of where resources are being applied across the County. By combining the strategic objectives of the individual departments and the County as a whole, and by linking program performance measurements with program costs, the budget can be used in the decision making process to cost effectively budget resources to meet the strategic objectives of the County.

D. List major services and programs provided by the department and set rank order priorities from highest to lowest.

E. Those agencies requesting computer hardware or software must submit a Computer Equipment request form issued by DOA - Budget and Information Systems divisions and, as prescribed within the County Code, obtain approval from the Manager of Information Systems on the appropriate forms prior to submission of the budget request to the Executive (See **Budget Instructions** for appropriate forms).

F. Inform the Public Works Department - Building Projects Manager of planned building and land improvements requests for consideration, prioritization, and inclusion into the County's five-year building improvement program plan or capital project plans.

G. Work with the administrators of internal service funds (and other operations that provide a service to other departments involving interdepartmental charges) to coordinate the levels of service and budget amounts necessary for the ensuing year.

H. Forward the completed sets of budget forms and supplemental information to the DOA - Budget Division.

I. Modify the budget request forms with any changes discussed and agreed upon with the DOA - Budget Division staff.

J. Present the department budget request to the County Executive at scheduled meeting(s). Prepare a written one page executive summary highlighting key policy issues and budget themes to begin presentation, highlight major points of each page of the department's budget document.

K. All tax levy departments are required to identify how expenditures are funded within the following categories:

　1. State funded mandates.

　2. State unfunded mandates.

　3. County funded programs.

　4. Program revenues and other funding.

L. Appear at standing/Finance Committee budget reviews, as requested, to present Executive's Budget or respond to Committee member's questions.

Exhibit 5-7 ■ Assignment of Budget Roles in the City of San Luis Obispo, California

The following summarizes roles and responsibilities for preparing, adopting and administering the Financial Plan:

- **City Council.** Sets goals; approves the Financial Plan and budget accordingly; makes changes to goals and resource allocations as necessary throughout the year. No expenditures are possible—from the lowliest paper clip to the most expensive CIP project—without an appropriation approved by the Council to do so.

- **Council Advisory Bodies.** Make recommendations to the Council as part of the goal-setting process; in some cases, review budget submissions before they are submitted to the Council.

- **City Administrative Officer (CAO).** Recommends the budget for Council consideration; ensures appropriate execution of the budget after adoption by the Council.

- **Department Heads.** Have the primary responsibility for assuring that: budget requests are fiscally conservative; budgets are prudently managed and executed after adoption by the Council; approved service levels are delivered at the lowest possible cost; budgets are well-researched, accurate, fully documented, and supported by the facts; budgets request funding levels necessary to deliver approved service levels, no more and no less; and that advisory bodies review budget proposals as appropriate.

- **Department Staff.** Participate with their department heads in carrying-out budget responsibilities as outlined above.

- **Department Fiscal Officers.** Coordinate departmental preparation of budgets.

- **Budget Review Team.** Reviews all budget requests and special review group recommendations; makes recommendations to the CAO. Members are:
  - Assistant CAO
  - Finance Director
  - Personnel Director
  - Budget Analysts

- **Budget Analysts.** Review department budget proposals as assigned to help ensure that they meet the CAO's standards as outlined under "Department Head" responsibilities above; review departmental budget trends with the CAO and Budget Review Team on a quarterly basis during the year. Assigned budget analysts are:
  - *Accounting Manager.* Public Works, Police, Fire
  - *Revenue Manager.* Utilities, Parks & Recreation
  - *Assistant to the CAO.* Administration, City Attorney, City Clerk, Personnel, Finance, Community Development

- **CIP Review Committee.** Reviews all CIP proposals and makes recommendations to the CAO. Members are:
  - Public Works Director, Chair
  - Utilities Director
  - Parks & Recreation Director
  - Finance Director
  - Community Development Director
  - Assistant to the CAO
  - Staff Support: City Engineer, Accounting Manager

Exhibit 5-7 ■ Assignment of Budget Roles in the City of San Luis Obispo, California (Continued)

- **General Fleet Coordinator.** Reviews all vehicle requests—for both new and replacement vehicles—before they are submitted to the CIP Review Committee and Budget Review Team.

- **Information Systems.** Reviews all significant operating program changes and CIP proposals affecting information technology before they are submitted to the CIP Review Committee and Budget Review Team.

- **Community Development Department.** Advises on CDBG eligibility and environmental issues; prepares CIP request for Mission Plaza improvements in accordance with Financial Plan policies that at least $50,000 be set aside annually for this purpose; schedules review of the CIP by the Planning Commission for General Plan consistency.

- **Public Works Department—Engineering Division.** Advises on CIP cost estimates and time-frames; establishes project schedules; manages construction projects and land acquisitions except in limited circumstances where the CAO has assigned project management responsibilities to another department on a case-by-case basis.

- **Finance Department.** Coordinates overall preparation of the Financial Plan; prepares and monitors revenue projections.

BUDGET PRACTICE 8.5—IDENTIFY OPPORTUNITIES FOR STAKEHOLDER INPUT

This budget practice recommends that governments provide opportunities in the budget process for obtaining stakeholder input. "Stakeholders" are anyone who is affected by or has a stake in the outcome of the budget. This may include citizens, customers of government services, elected officials, government management, government employees and unions, businesses, other governments, bondholders, and the media. The NACSLB recommends that the budget process include *all* stakeholders. Although the discussion in this section focuses on methods of obtaining *citizen* input, many of these methods can be applied to other stakeholder groups.

Obtaining stakeholder participation, and especially *citizen* participation, is important for several reasons. Citizen participation helps a government to be democratic and accountable to citizens. In addition, a better understanding of citizens' needs and priorities can improve a government's planning process. Citizen participation can also make it easier for government leaders to make difficult financial decisions (e.g., increasing taxes) if the community reaction has been tested beforehand in citizen forums. Further, a budget that is the product of sufficient citizen participation is more likely to gain community support when it is implemented. Finally, being responsive to citizen views can improve citizens' perceptions of government performance. In fact, a recent study in the *Journal of Public Budgeting, Accounting, & Financial Management* found that the <u>responsiveness</u> of the government is the single most important factor that shapes citizen's perceptions of local government performance. In other words, citizens that consider a government to be responsive (by demonstrating an interest in the views of citizens), also perceive that the government is performing well.[14]

Principles of Stakeholder Participation. The three principles for effective stakeholder participation in the budget process are: 1) good information for stakeholders, 2) early involvement by stakeholders, and 3) a government attitude that is open to participation.[15] Good information is necessary for citizens to understand the key budget issues. The budget format and the complexity of the budget document can affect the quality of citizen input. A line item format, for example, frustrates useful citizen input and focuses discussion on individual line items rather than how resources are allocated to community priorities. A lengthy document without an adequate summary also makes it difficult for citizens to see the "big picture". Involving stakeholders early in the budget process is also an important principle. Late involvement tends to make citizen involvement ineffective and negative in content because citizens are forced to respond to fully developed proposals, leaving no room for positive suggestions. Finally, it is important that government staff and leaders have an attitude that is open to citizen participation.

Methods of Stakeholder Participation. The methods of stakeholder participation in the budget process fall into three general categories: 1) better presentation of information, 2) informal stakeholder participation, and 3) formal stakeholder participation.

Better Presentation of Information. Several methods encourage and improve the quality of stakeholder participation by presenting budgetary information in a clear, easy to use format. These methods include:

- A well designed budget document using a budget format that facilitates evaluation (e.g., program or performance-based format);
- A budget summary or budget-in-brief;[16]
- Video presentations and cable TV broadcasts that summarize the budget;
- Newspaper inserts that summarize the budget document;
- Publishing budget information on a government web site;
- Budget simulators that demonstrate budget constraints;
- Presentations before interested groups.

Informal Stakeholder Participation. Informal participation refers to participation in the budget process by individuals or groups who do not have an official role in the process and have not been specially selected to participate. This is in contrast to methods of formal participation such as a citizen advisory committee. Methods of informal participation include:

- Citizen survey
- Letter writing
- Email
- Community meeting
- Public hearing

- Electronic community meeting
- Focus group
- Informal conversation
- Telephone
- Website chatroom

Formal Stakeholder Participation. Formal participation refers to participation in the budget process by individuals or groups who have an official role in the process and have been specially selected to participate. This is in contrast to methods of informal participation such as attending a public hearing or sending an email message. Methods of formal participation include advisory committees and formal input from community organizations.

Several methods of stakeholder participation are highlighted below. The first method, video presentations, is one effective way to present budget information. Public hearings are a common method of obtaining stakeholder input in most governments. Electronic community meetings are an effective way to make participating in budget discussions more convenient for citizens. Citizen surveys solicit input from a representative sample of citizens, not just the most vocal ones. Finally, citizen advisory committees—composed of citizens who commit time to studying budget issues—provide a way to solicit *well-informed* citizen input.

Video Presentations. One innovative method of summarizing budget information is to present it in a video format. A budget video can be an effective way to communicate complex financial information in a way that is easy to understand. The video media is one of the most popular ways that people in our culture receive information. Many citizens who would never read a budget document might watch a budget video on the local cable television station. Another distinct advantage that the video media has over printed media is that it is possible to show *visually* what the money is being spent on. For example, instead of simply showing the expenditures for a graffiti removal program, a budget video could include a video clip of city workers removing graffiti.

Several suggestions[17] for an effective budget video include:

- A strong opening which presents a meaningful message, sending a signal to listeners that the information being presented will be what they need to know to make informed decisions.

- Hone the essence of the message down. While 20 minutes usually is maximum for most oral presentations, a videotape never should exceed 10 minutes.

- To achieve a receptive audience, a high level of preparation is necessary. Offer a precise overview providing the essential facts in language that nonfinance people can understand.

- The audience's needs come first; the presenter's last. Audiences basically are seeking two things: to understand the message and to feel good about their decision. Remember Voltaire's remark, "The secret to being a bore is to tell everything."

- Stick to the point and cut whatever can be cut. A useful formula for a successful budget presentation is to select a good beginning and a good ending, then try to keep them as close together as possible.

- Using big numbers is another frequent error. The nonfinancial listeners may not easily digest large number such as $75 million or $100 billion; they may perceive it as "padded" or as having no meaning to them in terms of their own lives. Relate large numbers to the audience's own pocketbook or wallet.

- Another hostility-generating technique is the use of too many acronyms. Avoid them when possible or explain them at the beginning of the presentation.

Public Hearings. Most governments conduct public hearings to obtain input from citizens and other stakeholders. In fact, many state statutes and local ordinances require a public hearing on the budget. Typically, public hearings are held late in the budget process after a proposed budget has been produced. However, citizen input has the greatest effect when it is obtained early in the budget process. In addition, citizen input tends to be more positive in character (i.e., suggestions rather than criticisms) when it is obtained early in the process. For this reason, some governments hold a "pre-budget" public hearing early in the budget process in addition to a regular hearing to review the proposed budget. The purpose of a pre-budget hearing is to receive suggestions on projects that should be considered in planning the upcoming budget.

Electronic Community Meeting. An electronic community meeting is a televised forum with elected leaders and government staff in which viewers can phone-in questions or comments while they are watching the program. Compared to other methods of stakeholder participation such as public hearings, an electronic meeting format makes participation very convenient for citizens. Citizens are able to participate from their homes without having to travel to a government facility and without having to sacrifice the time required to sit through an entire hearing. In addition, phoning in comments to staff is less intimidating than speaking in a public hearing.

The City of Fitchburg, Wisconsin used an electronic meeting format to solicit ideas and develop a vision for the community' future. During the meeting, city department heads gave brief summaries and citizens participated with questions and comments by phoning into the program or by speaking from the live audience. Caller's responses were read aloud by the moderator or broadcast live on the program. Staff recorded responses on easels placed around the room (see Exhibit 5-8).[18]

Several suggestions[19] for an effective electronic community meeting include:

- Work with local schools and media to promote participation at the meeting.
- Make it lively—have a high energy moderator who reminds viewers that even if someone else already has called in about an issue, they also should call to emphasize it.
- Have a practice session to work through any technology bugs that may occur. Begin working with the telephone company at least three months in advance of the meeting to make sure the phone system can handle the volume of calls.
- Keep the meeting to two hours in length. Hold it in the early evening on a date that does not conflict with local sporting or cultural events (preferable a weekday).
- Invite government representatives and local community groups to participate. Have your audience warmed up prior to going live—the moderator should walk them through what the meeting will be like and ask some of the participants to write down their issues.

Citizen Surveys. A citizen survey is a series of questions administered to a relatively large representative sample of the population. There are three major types of surveys: mailed questionnaires, tele-

Exhibit 5-8 ■ Electronic Community Meeting Setup

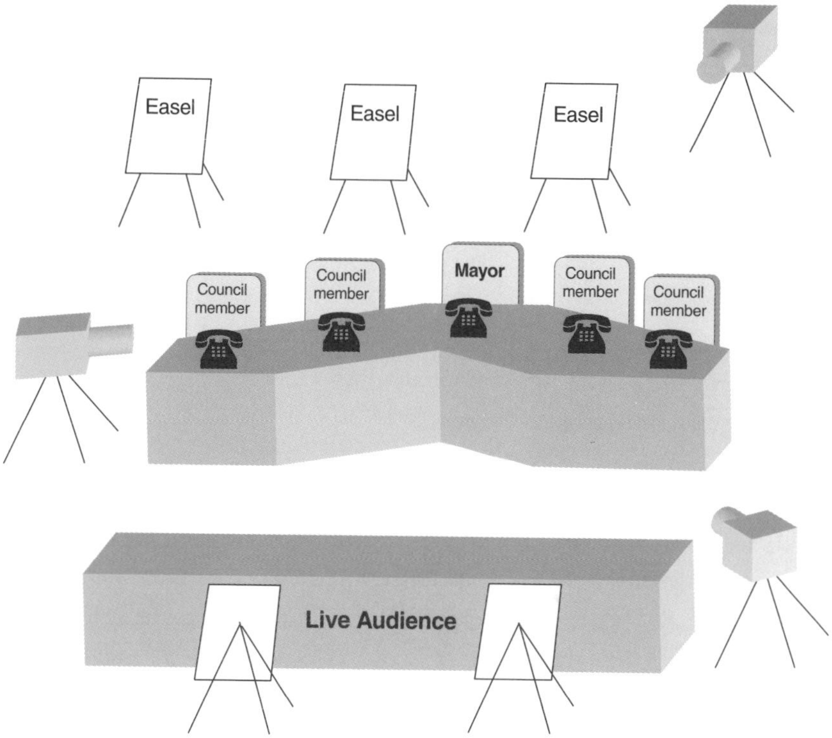

phone interviews, and in person interviews.[20] Surveys are frequently used to identify citizen priorities and measure citizens' perceptions of the effectiveness of government services. An important difference between surveys and most other methods of stakeholder participation is that surveys include input from a representative sample of the population, not just the most vocal or politically active citizens. A typical process for conducting a citizen survey is shown in Exhibit 5-9.[21]

Survey designers have identified a number of best practices in conducting citizen surveys.[23] These practices include:

1. Define objectives for the survey which are specific, clear-cut, and unambiguous.
2. Define the target population for the survey, and a sampling frame that adequately represents the target population.

Exhibit 5-9 ■ The Citizen Survey Process[22]

1. Identify the focus of the study and method of research;
2. Determine the research schedule and budget;
3. Establish an information base;
4. Determine the sampling frame;
5. Determine the sample size and sample selection procedures;
6. Design the survey instrument;
7. Pretest the survey instrument;
8. Select and train interviewers;
9. Implement the survey;
10. Code the completed questionnaires and computerize the data; and,
11. Analyze the data and prepare the final report.

---

3. Use random probability sampling to draw a representative sample of the target population.

4. Select the best approach to data collection (e.g., face-to-face interviews, telephone surveys, and mail surveys).

5. Design a questionnaire that avoids bias in the wording and order of questions.

6. Design questions that use appropriate types of performance indicators. For example, the questions in citizen surveys should not ask citizens to rate their general satisfaction with a particular service, but should be targeted at specific aspects of service provision (e.g., responsiveness, courtesy of staff, and amount of paperwork required). In addition, the survey should omit any questions concerning matters for which the government has no control. Further, citizens should only be asked questions concerning events within their own personal experience (or of other members of their household). They should not be asked technical questions.

7. Pretest the survey questionnaire to detect potential problems such as:

- Long, awkwardly worded, or ambiguous questions,
- Local language usage that requires a special choice of words,

- Confusing or incorrect instructions to interviewers regarding "skip" patterns,
- Redundant questions,
- Wording that may offend or sound foolish to respondents,
- Illogical or awkward sequence of questions,
- Difficulties encountered by interviewers in recording responses,
- Inappropriate response categories.
8. Correctly assess the extent to which the sample is representative of the target population.
9. Use interviewers with adequate training and supervision. Sample a percentage of the interviews to verify the quality of survey data.
10. Recognize that opinions are sometimes provided even when a respondent does not have an opinion.
11. Report survey results in an unbiased fashion.
12. Acquire the services of a professional survey research firm.

Advisory Committees. A citizen advisory committee is a group of citizens who have been specially selected to have an official role in the budget process. Typically, an advisory committee will meet early in the budget process to suggest priorities, and will also meet at various times during the process and late in the process to review the proposed budget. Governments use various methods to select citizens to serve on advisory committees including: appointment by the mayor, appointment by the city manager with council approval, and election. Governments usually provide their advisory committees with technical and clerical support, and sometimes provide funding that enables the committees to hire their own independent staff. Advisory committees generally receive greater access to timely, high-quality government information, and in some cases, receive neighborhood-specific data.

Advisory committees have several important advantages as a method of stakeholder participation. Most importantly, advisory committees provide a way of obtaining *informed* citizen input. Committee members have greater access to information and more time and interest to learn about the government's budget issues. Committees can also provide a fresh perspective on issues and a source of ideas and suggestions to improve the government. Membership on an advisory committee can force interest groups to take less of a parochial view and more of a perspective of what is best for the community as a whole. When proposals are being formulated, citizen committees can provide a way to test citizens' response to government proposals (such as tax increases and service cutbacks) early in the budget process. Finally, including community leaders on an advisory committee can create important supporters who can strengthen the implementation of the adopted budget.

Potential Problems with Stakeholder Participation. It is crucial to be aware of several potential problems with stakeholder participation. Some methods of citizen participation tend to obtain input only from the most vocal or politically active citizens. This input may be unrepresentative of the community as a whole. Another major problem is that, even if input is obtained from a broader group of citizens, those citizens may be uninformed. For example, citizens may state that the government needs more police because they are unaware of a recent increase in the size of the police force. In addition, many citizens do not have the time and interest to understand complex budgeting and financial matters so they may take positions that are actually not in their best interests. For example, citizens may support a tax cut even though it could lead to service reductions and more costly borrowing. Finally, from the point of view of the government, including citizens in the budget process can consume time and funds and can generate embarrassment if mistakes are discovered.

Solution: Multiple Methods of Stakeholder Participation. A solution to many of the potential problems of stakeholder participation is to use a combination of several participation methods. For example, by using both a citizen survey and a citizen advisory committee, a government could address the problem of unrepresentative input with the survey and the problem of uninformed citizen input with the citizen advisory committee.

Citizen surveys are an excellent way to obtain citizen input that is representative of the community as a whole. Electronic community meetings are also a good way to encourage more citizen participation.

Citizen advisory committees are an excellent way to address the problem of *uninformed* citizen input because they are composed of a group of citizens who devote their time and energy to understanding budget issues. Another way to address the problem of uninformed citizen input is to improve the presentation of budgetary information and create better informed citizens through methods such as budget-in-brief publications, video presentations, and newspaper inserts. Appendix C shows how the cities of Winnipeg, Ontario, Cincinnati, Ohio, and Dayton, Ohio have used multiple methods of citizen participation.[24]

Selecting Methods of Stakeholder Participation. The three major criteria for selecting methods of stakeholder participation are: political acceptability, effectiveness, and feasibility.[25] Political acceptability is the extent to which stakeholders and government leaders consider the method to be fair. Effectiveness is the extent to which the method does a good job at obtaining informed input from a representative group of stakeholders. Feasibility is extent to which the costs of the method are worth the benefits, and whether stakeholders will likely possess the time and interest necessary to participate. Exhibit 5-10 summarizes methods of stakeholder participation.

Exhibit 5-11 compares citizen input methods based on the number of citizens that provide comments and the quality and detail of those comments. This exhibit shows that citizen surveys involve the most citizens, but also tends to solicit brief responses. On the other end of the spectrum, advisory committees generate detailed input, but involve a small number of citizens.

Current Use of Various Methods of Stakeholder Participation. Currently, the most widely used methods of stakeholder participation are public hearings and budget summaries. Methods such as group presentations and advisory committees are used by about one-third of local governments. Other methods are used less frequently. Exhibit 5-12 shows the prevalence of citizen input mechanisms in local governments.

SUMMARY

This chapter discussed how to implement four NACSLB budget practices related to the organization of the budget function and the assignment of roles and responsibilities in the budget process. The discussion covered the following NACSLB budget practices:

- Practice 8.1—Develop a Budget Calendar;
- Practice 8.2—Develop Budget Guidelines and Instructions;

Exhibit 5-10 ■ Methods of Stakeholder Participation

Method	Description	Strengths of Method
Better Presentation of Information		
Well designed budget document	A printed budget document in a clear, easy-to-use format using a budget format that facilitates evaluation (e.g., a program or performance-based format)	• Provides stakeholders with complete information on the government's finances and operations.
Printed budget summaries	A condensed summary of the budget document.	• Provides brief information for citizens with a casual interest in the budget. • Informs a large number of citizens at a low cost.
Video presentations	A presentation that uses the video format to summarize budget information. The video may be broadcast on a local cable television station or shown to community groups.	• Provides brief information for citizens with a casual interest in the budget. • Informs a large number of citizens at a low cost. • Television is one of the most popular ways that citizens receive information. • Can show visually what government money is spent on.
Newspaper insert	A summary of budget information in an insert to a local newspaper.	• Provides brief information for citizens with a casual interest in the budget. • Informs a large number of citizens at a low cost.
Web site	Publishing budget information and budget document on government web site.	• Low cost method of distribution. • Very convenient for citizens.
Budget simulators	A computer program that enables citizens to see the result of hypothetical spending and taxing scenarios. May be accessed through the government's web site.	• Can be used to educate citizens about the zero-sum nature of budgeting.
Oral presentations	Oral presentations of budget information before interested community groups.	• Good for emphasizing major budget issues. • Can tailor presentation to a specific group.

Exhibit 5-10 ■ Methods of Stakeholder Participation (Continued)

Method	Description	Strengths of Method
Informal Stakeholder Participation		
Citizen opinion surveys	A series of questions administered to a relatively large representative sample of the population.	• Can be used to measure the effectiveness of services and to identify citizen priorities. • Input is from a representative sample of all citizens, not just the most vocal or politically active.
Letter writing	Citizens are encouraged to send letters to elected officials or budget staff.	• Citizen input likely to be well structured and thought out.
Email	Citizens are encouraged to send email messages to elected officials or budget staff.	• Convenience and less intimidating form of communication encourages citizens to participate.
Community meetings	Government officials meet with citizens at various locations in the community (e.g., school auditorium) to solicit community input.	• Conveniently located, informal setting encourages citizen participation.
Public hearings	Citizens make comments at an official government meeting, typically in a government setting.	• Provides an opportunity for citizen participation.
Electronic community meetings	A televised forum with elected leaders and government staff in which viewers can phone-in questions or comments while they are watching the program.	• Very convenient for citizens to participate. • Phoning in a response is less intimidating than speaking in a public hearing.
Citizen focus groups	A structured discussion led by a trained facilitator.	• Obtaining an in-depth understanding of citizen views that cannot be captured by a survey. • Can have follow up questions. • Inexpensive and fast method of surveying citizens.
Informal conversations	In-person discussions with elected officials or budget staff.	• Excellent method for answering questions and clarifying budget issues.
Telephone	Citizens are encouraged to call elected officials or budget staff.	• Excellent method for answering questions and clarifying budget issues.
Web site chatroom	Citizens are encouraged to participate in a chatroom forum on the government's Web site.	• Very convenient for citizens to participate. • Participating in a chat room is much less intimidating than speaking in a public hearing.

Exhibit 5-10 ■ Methods of Stakeholder Participation (Continued)

Method	Description	Strengths of Method
Formal Stakeholder Participation		
Advisory committee	A group of citizens who have been specially selected to have an official role in the budget process.	• Provides a way of obtaining *informed* citizen input. • Provides a fresh perspective on issues and a source of ideas and suggestions to improve the government. • Membership on an advisory committee can force interest groups to take less of a parochial view and more of a perspective of what is best for the community as a whole. • Provides a way to test citizens' response to government proposals early in the budget process. • Can create important supporters who can strengthen the implementation of the adopted budget.
Formal input from community organizations	Existing community organizations are selected to submit formal input into the budget process (e.g., requests for new programs and projects).	• Provides a way of obtaining *informed* citizen input. • Provides a fresh perspective on issues and a source of ideas and suggestions to improve the government.

Exhibit 5-11 ■ Comparing Citizen Input Methods

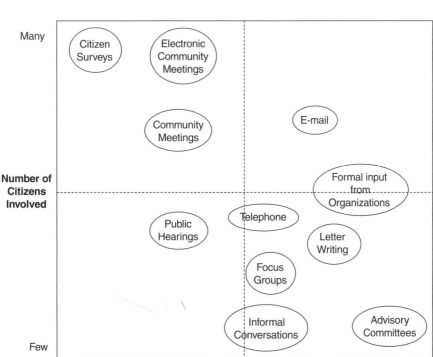

- Practice 8.3—Develop Mechanisms for Coordinating Budget Preparation and Review;
- Practice 8.5—Identify Opportunities for Stakeholder Input.

These practices focus on the administrative structure and coordination tools that governments should have in place to facilitate an effective budget process.

Exhibit 5-12 ■ Current Use of Various Citizen Input Mechanisms[26]

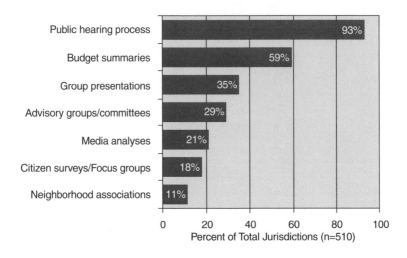

Percent of Total Jurisdictions (n=510)

- Public hearing process — 93%
- Budget summaries — 59%
- Group presentations — 35%
- Advisory groups/committees — 29%
- Media analyses — 21%
- Citizen surveys/Focus groups — 18%
- Neighborhood associations — 11%

Endnotes

1. This list is adapted from Juliet Carol Powdar, *The Operating Budget: A Guide for Smaller Governments* (Chicago: Government Finance Officers Association, 1996), 32.
2. Source: Volusia County, Florida—Budget Document, D-10.
3. Source: City of Glendale, Arizona—*Budget Process Training Manual*, "Budget Preparation Checklist," 18.
4. This section is based on *The Operating Budget*, 38-40.
5. This section is adapted from *The Operating Budget*, 39-40.
6. Source: Jackson County, Oregon—*Budget Preparation Manual*.
7. This section is adapted from *The Operating Budget*, 9-11.
8. *The Operating Budget*, 11.
9. Daniel E. O'Toole, James Marshall, and Timothy Grewe, "Current Local Government Budgeting Practices," *Government Finance Review* 12 (December 1996): 25-29.
10. GFOA Research and Consulting Center survey, August 2000.
11. O'Toole, et al.
12. Source: City of Scottsdale, Arizona—*Biennial Budget*.
13. Source: Waukesha County, Wisconsin, "Financial Procedures Manual."
14. Mark A. Glaser and Robert B. Denhardt, "Local Government Performance Through the Eyes of Citizens," *Journal of Public Budgeting, Accounting, & Financial Management*, Spring 2000, 12 (1), 49-73.
15. This discussion is based on Michael J. Meshenberg, *Municipal Budgeting in Chicago: Who Cares What the People Think?* (Chicago: Center for Economic Policy Analysis, 1989).
16. For further information see the following GFOA Recommended Practices: "Providing a Concise Summary of the Budget (1996)," and "Use of Financial Status in the Budget Process (1999)." For an excellent example of a budget-in-brief that also serves as an educational document on local government budgeting, see the *Taxpayer's Guide to the Hillsborough County Budget*. This document is produced by the Hillsborough County, Florida Budget Department.
17. This list is taken from James G. Scharret and Barbara Bartos, "Communicating Financial Information: Southfield's Financial Public Relations," *Government Finance Review* 7 (April 1991): 22.

18. This exhibit is based on a diagram from Norma DeHaven, "Connecting With Taxpayers: The Electronic Town Hall Meeting," *Government Finance Review* 15 (October 1999): 49.
19. Ibid.
20. Web site surveys are another method for conducting citizen surveys.
21. The ICMA publication, *Citizen Surveys: How to Do Them, How to Use Them, What They Mean, Second Edition*, is an excellent resource on this topic.
22. Based on Louis M. Rea and Richard A. Parker, *Designing and Conducting Survey Research: A Comprehensive Guide* (San Francisco: Jossey-Bass Publishers, 1997).
23. This list is based on Michael W. Link and Robert W. Oldendick, "The Role of Survey Research in the Benchmarking Process," *Journal of Public Budgeting, Accounting, & Financial Management*, Spring 2000, 12 (1), 138-164; and Harry Hatry, et al., *How Effective Are Your Community Services?* (Washington, DC: ICMA & Urban Institute), 215-225.
24. For an excellent article that highlights the multiple methods of stakeholder participation used in Hillsborough County, Florida see Eric R. Johnson, "Recommended Budget Practices: Incorporating Stakeholders into the Process," *Government Finance Review* 14 (August 1998): 15-18.
25. This discussion of criteria is based on Meshenberg, 1989.
26. O'Toole, et al., Exhibit 5, 28.

Budget Office Names

This appendix shows the names given to budget offices in large U.S. cities, categorized by the location of the budget office in the government organization.

Freestanding Budget Offices

Name	City
Budget Department	Detroit
Budget Department	Mobile
Budget Division	St. Louis
Budget Office	Arlington
Budget & Finance Agency	Oakland
Office of Budget and Financial Analysis	Colorado Springs
Finance & Budget Department	Louisville
Financial Management Department	San Diego
Budget & Research Department	Phoenix
Budget and Research	Tucson
Budget and Evaluation	Charlotte
Budget and Management Studies Division	Fresno
Budget and Strategic Planning	Richmond
Bureau of Budget and Efficiency	Rochester
Budget and Management Department	St. Petersburg

Office of Budget and Management	Chicago
Department of Management & Budget	Miami
Office of Management and Budget	Corpus Christi
Office of Management and Budget	El Paso
Office of Management and Budget	San Antonio
Department of Management Services	Virginia Beach

Budget Offices in a Chief Executive's Office

Chief Executive's Office	Name of Budget Subunit	City
Chief Administrative Officer	Office of Management and Budget	Albuquerque
Chief Administrative Officer	Budget Office	New Orleans
City Administrative Officer	Budget Formulation and Control	Los Angeles
City Manager	Budget Office	Bakersfield
City Manager	Office of Management and Budget	Kansas City
City Manager	Budget Office	Riverside
City Manager	Budget Office	San Jose
City Manager	(no designated budget unit)	Stockton
City Manager's Office	Budget Office	Fort Worth
Municipal Manager	Office of Management and Budget	Anchorage
Executive Services	City Budget Office	Seattle
Mayor's Office	Office of Management and Budget	Pittsburgh
Mayor's Office	Office of Budget & Legislative Affairs	San Francisco

Budget Offices in an Administration Department

Administration Department	Name of Budget Subunit	City
Management Services	Budget & Research Division	Mesa
Department of Administration	Budget & Management Division	Milwaukee
Administrative Services	Budgeting Division	Lexington-Fayette
Administrative Services	Office of Management and Budget	Newark
Administrative Services	(no designated budget unit)	Raleigh
Administrative Services	Budget & Policy Review Division	Sacramento
Administration & Finance	Budget Division	Jacksonville

Administration and Finance	Budget Office	Buffalo
Office of Finance & Administration	Bureau of Financial Planning	Portland
Finance & Business Services	Budget & Finance Division	Las Vegas
Finance & Management Services	Budget Division	Santa Ana
Finance and Administration Department	Budget & Evaluation Division	Houston
Finance and Administrative Services	City Budget Office	Austin

Budget Offices in a Finance Department

Finance Department	Name of Budget Subunit	City
Finance	Audit and Budget	Akron
Finance	Budget Division	Anaheim
Finance	Bureau of Budget & Management Analysis	Atlanta
Finance	Office of Budget & Financial Planning	Aurora
Finance	Bureau of Budget and Management Research	Baltimore
Finance	Budgeting Division	Baton Rouge
Finance	Budget Division	Birmingham
Finance	Office of Budget Management	Boston
Finance	Budget and Evaluation Division	Cincinnati
Finance	Financial Management Section	Columbus
Finance	Office of Management and Budget	Nashville
Finance	Office of Management and Budget	Oklahoma City
Finance	Budget and Accounting	Omaha
Finance	Administration and Budget	Santa Monica
Finance	Office of Budget & Research	Wichita
Finance Office	Budget & Management Office	Denver
Finance Department	Budget Office	Lincoln
Finance Department	Financial Services & Budget Division	Minneapolis
Finance Department	OMB	Cleveland
Finance Department	Budget Bureau	Philadelphia
Finance Department	Budget & Planning Division	Tulsa
Division of Finance	Budget Office	Memphis
Financial Management	Budget Management Bureau	Long Beach

Financial Services Office	Budget Section	St. Paul
Office of Financial Services	Operating Budget Division	Dallas
Office of the Chief Financial Officer	Office of Management and Budget	Washington
Office of the City Controller	(no designated budget unit)	Indianapolis
Budget and Fiscal Services Department	Financial Policy, Planning, & Analysis	Honolulu
Revenue and Finance	Budget Division	Tampa

Development and Training Resources for Budget Analysts

Category	Skills	GFOA Resources
Understand Government's Finances and Operations	• Budget process and procedures outlined in budget manual. • Goal-setting and policy formation process. • Expenditure and revenue structure and debt financing. • Fund accounting, government's chart of accounts, and government's internal and external financial reports. • Proficiency with government's financial management system and desktop applications. • Knowledge of the operating departments that the analyst has responsibility over	GFOA Seminars • Budgeting for Budget Analysts GFOA Publications • The Operating Budget: A Guide for Smaller Governments • Local Government Finance: Concepts and Practices
People Skills, Political Skills	• Interpersonal skills • Persuasion/marketing skills • Political savvy • Negotiation skills • Interviewing skills • Conflict resolution skills. • Oral and written communication skills.	GFOA Seminars • Budgeting for Budget Analysts • Intermediate Governmental Budgeting • Bargaining and Negotiation Skills for Finance Officers

| Financial and Policy Analysis Skills | **Analytical concepts:** adjusting for inflation, time value of money and discounting to present value, unit cost, sunk cost, opportunity cost, fixed and variable cost, differential cost, marginal cost, basic statistics

Proficiency with analysis tools and techniques:
• Basic techniques for comparing alternatives: decision tables, expected value tables, weighted score tables, decision trees;
• Advanced analytical techniques: break-even analysis, net present value analysis, return on investment analysis, cost-benefit analysis, fiscal impact analysis, cost-effectiveness analysis, sensitivity analysis;
• Expenditure and revenue analysis and forecasting;
• Financial condition analysis – ICMA Financial Trend Monitoring System, 10 point test of financial condition.
• Performance measurement – systematic, regular, government-wide
• Program evaluation – focused on particular program, in-depth, ad hoc
• Management analysis – analysis of work methods and organization; Service delivery planning and innovations
• Capital improvement programming – Assess capital needs, assess financial capacity including debt capacity, evaluate potential capital projects, plan projects and funding, develop capital budget, implement and monitor capital budget.
• Understand cost accounting and cost analysis | GFOA Publications
• Decision Tools for Budgetary Analysis
• Priority-Setting Models for Public Budgeting
• Revenue Analysis and Forecasting
• An Elected Official's Guide to Performance Measurement
• Implementing Performance Measurement in Government: Illustrations and Resources
• Benchmarking and Measuring Debt Capacity
• Capital Improvement Programming: A Guide for Smaller Governments

GFOA Seminars
• Budgeting for Budget Analysts
• Financial Planning and Forecasting
• Introduction to Performance Measurement
• Performance Measurement II
• Costing Government Services
• Capital Budgeting and Finance |

| Familiarity with Innovations in Budgeting | • NACSLB recommended practices
• GFOA Budget Awards program
• GFOA Recommended Practices
• Long-term financial planning, multi-year budgeting, budgeting for structural balance
• Strategic planning
• Alternative budget formats: program, performance, zero-based budgets | GFOA Publications
• Best Practices in Public Budgeting: Narratives and Illustrations on CD-ROM
• Recommended Budget Practices: A Framework for Improved State and Local Government Budgeting
• Recommended Practices for State and Local Governments (GFOA)
• Budget Awards Program: Illustrations and Examples of Program Criteria
• An Elected Official's Guide to Multi-Year Budgeting
• Budgeting for High Performance Organizations: New Models and Best Practices (Video)

GFOA Seminars
• Best Practices in Budgeting
• Budgeting for Budget Analysts
• GFOA Annual Conference sessions on Budgeting and Financial Planning |

For information on GFOA publications and seminars contact the GFOA at 312-977-9700, www.gfoa.org

Using Multiple Methods of Citizen Participation

This appendix shows three examples of governments that use multiple methods to obtain citizen participation in the budget process.

THE COMMUNITY CONSULTATION PROCESS IN THE CITY OF WINNIPEG, ONTARIO[1]

From November 1999 to January 2000, the City of Winnipeg conducted an extensive community consultation process with citizens and organizations in the City of Winnipeg. This community input will form the basis of a five-year financial plan to be released later in 2000. The objectives of the community consultation were to:

- inform the citizens of Winnipeg about the financial status of the City and review options being considered, to achieve tax cuts over the next five years; provide an opportunity for the citizens of Winnipeg to have significant input into the long range financial planning of the City;
- identify key issues raised by the citizens of Winnipeg regarding property tax reductions, user fees, core services, service quality, alternative service-delivery and Provincial government cost-sharing.

The consultation process consisted of six components. It was designed to provide a variety of options for community participation and sought both quantitative and qualitative information from citizens and organizations.

Focus Groups: At the beginning of the consultation process four professionally facilitated focus groups were conducted. The focus groups explored citizen opinions of the most critical civic issues to be addressed by the Mayor and Council, interpretations of a 10% tax cut and the implications of implementing property tax reductions.

Telephone Survey: Following the completion of the focus groups, a comprehensive telephone survey was conducted with 400 residents of Winnipeg. The telephone survey determined citizen opinion of the most important civic issues to be addressed by the Mayor and Council, the importance and performance of various City services and the acceptability of different options to achieve property tax reductions.

Information Booklet: In the middle of December 1999 a nine-page information booklet, entitled "Achieving Affordable Government: Community Consultation Background Towards a 10% Tax Cut," was distributed by Canada Post to all households in Winnipeg. The booklet informed citizens of the various issues and options around achieving affordable government and property tax reductions. The booklet contained sections on Understanding the City Budget, Reducing the Cost of City Government, Government Cost Sharing, Alternative Revenue Strategies and Additional Long-Term Strategies. As well, the booklet listed all the community consultation events with dates, locations and a telephone number and Web site to contact for more information.

Community Forum: Citizens and organizations were encouraged to submit written briefs for presentation at the Community Forum held at the Museum of Man and Nature Auditorium on January 10 and 11, 2000. The forum gave citizens and organizations an opportunity to present their ideas and positions in a more formal and comprehensive way. The forum was extended to two days due to overwhelming response. Thirty-six verbal presentations of the written briefs were made to Mayor Murray and other city councilors and senior administrators at the forum.

Community Workshops: Six Community Workshops, hosted by Mayor Murray, were held at community centres in various sections of Winnipeg. The workshops provided citizens with a factual overview of the City's financial challenges and an opportunity to participate in discussions about options for achieving affordable government and a property tax reduction.

Online 4uwinnipegcom Survey: Upon mailing of the Information Booklet a website was launched by *4uwinnipeg.com Online Business Directory.* The site provided an opportunity for citizens to participate and express ideas on their own time and in the comfort of their own homes or offices. The site included all the contents of the Information Booklet and provided links to Mayor Murray's budget discussion paper which contained more comprehensive information. The site also posed twelve questions about various options for achieving affordable government for visitors to respond to.

STAKEHOLDER PARTICIPATION IN THE CITY OF CINCINNATI, OHIO[2]

In Cincinnati, city government solicits budget advice from the public in several systematic ways:

1. Help with setting citywide goals and objectives early in the process comes from an annual Citizen Budget Assembly (CBA) convened by the city manager, and from community surveys conducted every few years.

2. Specific requests for projects are solicited from community councils which submit Community Budget Requests (CBRS) each year.

3. The city council holds a central public hearing and several neighborhood hearings.

Information from these sources is specifically considered by city officials as they prepare the annual operating, capital, and CDBG budgets.

Public participation begins each year shortly after the previous year's appropriation ordinance is adopted by the city council. At the end of May, six months before council adoption, the CBA is convened and CBRs are due from community councils.

Both processes began around 1985 as a result of concern by the mayor and chairman of the council finance committee that citizens had little interest in budget issues. They conceived the notion of the two-level approach and implemented it immediately.

The CBA meets in a structured two- to five-hour forum to advise the city early in the budget cycle on overall objectives and priorities. Participation is by invitation. Invitations are sent to community activists, as well as leaders of special interest and civic groups with an effort made to obtain geographic and interest balance. Over 60 people attended the 1989 assembly. Preliminary city plans are presented and participants break into groups to discuss particular issues. Key city officials attend as resource people.

The results of the CBA are used to help city officials develop the objectives that guide budget preparation, e.g., needs requiring special attention, new programs, revised priority rankings.

Concurrently with preparations for the CBA, the Department of Research, Evaluation and Budget (REB) solicits CBRs from each of the city's 50 community-councils. These are general-purpose neighborhood-based grass-roots organizations. Forms are sent out asking each organization to identify and prioritize five projects that it wants the city to fund. Projects may be either service or capital and must represent an official request from each organization.

Organizations develop their requests by holding community assemblies and requesting ideas from block clubs, local special interest groups, or individuals. Technical help is made available by REB, the Department of Neighborhood Housing and Conservation, and other departments. Each department has liaisons who work with neighborhood leaders before and during the budget preparation process. They may offer advice on the likelihood of success of particular proposals, assist with cost estimation, and explain how to fill out forms.

Cincinnati's 50 neighborhoods each are served by a community council that receives general fund support—up to $10,000—through a neighborhood support program. Organizations are recognized by inclusion in the annual ordinance funding the program. Funding requests from other groups must be funneled through the local councils, although lobbying of city officials or council members occurs outside the formal CBR process.

CBRs are received by REB in late May and are routed to the appropriate city department for review. Each request must receive a response. If rejected, reasons must be given. If accepted, the request becomes part of the department's submission to REB.

Approximately 42 of the 50 community councils have participated in recent years, each submitting up to five requests…. In effect, city officials report, CBRs are treated the same as requests from any city department, accepted or rejected by departments and the city manager on their merits based on available funds.

A final means to obtain public input is through a periodic random survey sponsored by the city. Conducted about every 3-4 years, the city hires a university survey center to poll Cincinnati residents on problems, city services, and funding priorities. Costing $20-30,000, these surveys are used to check city officials' own opinions and the comments obtained in the Citizen Budget Assembly.

Overall, the Cincinnati approach is an attempt to develop a cooperative effort in budgeting between the city administration, city council, civic groups, and neighborhood-based organizations. The city has not determined the full cost of these efforts, but they are not inexpensive. In Cincinnati, they consider the expenditures well worth it. City officials and the bureaucracy are sensitized to community concerns and the public has a direct voice in setting objectives and selecting projects.

STAKEHOLDER PARTICIPATION IN THE CITY OF DAYTON, OHIO[3]

Because of its extensive participation and information collection process, and because of its innovations in presentation of budgets and program strategies, Dayton, frequently is mentioned in literature about local government as a national leader in financial planning and public participation. It has developed an array of mechanisms to annually evaluate agency performance as a basis for setting its budget priorities for the coming year and to plan for future years. The public is involved at virtually every step of the way.

Public involvement occurs in two major ways. First, seven "priority boards" covering the entire city have been established as a formal, ongoing feedback mechanism for city officials (six serve neighborhoods and one the central business district). Second, the city conducts an annual independent survey of resident opinion about service delivery and community conditions. These mechanisms have been in place for about ten years….

Priority boards. In contrast to Cincinnati, Dayton's priority boards do not submit formal requests for service projects to City Hall, although they do submit capital project requests. Rather, through a series of systematic steps, they work with city officials to identify needs and provide feedback on how the city is doing in meeting those needs, including evaluating the service performance of the 19 city departments.

To facilitate development of a systematic and orderly citizen input process, the city commission passed an informal resolution in 1975 recognizing the priority boards as the principal citizen participation vehicle in budgeting, CDBG funding, and monitoring municipal services.

Each priority board has 30-40 members elected annually by the registered voters in the district. Election procedures are locally determined and vary among the districts. Each year they prepare and submit a needs statement detailing the board's assessment of neighborhood conditions, service provided, and service and project improvement needs. Information is collected via surveys, community hearings, interaction with community groups, and other means.

Acting through their chairpersons, the boards serve as the official voice for their neighborhoods, identifying needs, communicating problems, disseminating information, and assessing service effectiveness. Priority board chairpeople meet monthly with the city manager and each board meets regularly with a neighborhood "administrative council" of middle managers from city agencies. The city also provides on-site professional staff for each priority board. Currently, there are 27 city staff positions serving the seven boards.

Annually, on a regular schedule, priority boards evaluate how well their previously identified needs have been met. This process includes identifying any new needs that may have emerged and is one of the first steps in the city's overall goal-setting. Board reports are reviewed by city staff which may respond by: (a) accepting the items as part of the city's work plan, (b) holding further discussions with the boards, or (c) considering more systematic solutions, particularly for citywide problems. Departments are required to formally respond to neighborhood needs statements.

Priority boards supplement rather than replace conventional community organizations. The traditional organizations appear to have only limited interest in budget matters; as in Cincinnati, these concerns tend to be directed to the priority boards where they can receive a more sympathetic hearing, than to city officials directly.

Public opinion survey. The public opinion survey is conducted each August, with approximately 900 residents polled for their views on a wide variety of topics ranging from neighborhood safety to government effectiveness. The city has used public funds to contract with local universities or private marketing firms to conduct the surveys.

Senior city staff offer suggestions on what should be included in the survey. Final suggestions are included in a request for proposals for a contractor. After the poll is completed, OMB reviews the results and distributes information to appropriate departments. This approach has often helped identify new and emerging issues which are used in establishing long-term strategies and short-term department performance objectives.

Endnotes

1. Source: *Achieving Affordable Government: Community Consultation Towards a 10% Tax Cut Report* (City of Winnipeg, February 2000), 7-8.
2. Taken from Michael J. Meshenberg, *Municipal Budgeting in Chicago: Who Cares What the People Think?* (Chicago: Center for Economic Policy Analysis, 1989), 36-38.
3. Taken from Meshenberg, 39-41.